BOOKS FOR SCHOOLS: IMPROVING ACCESS TO SUPPLEMENTARY READING MATERIALS IN AFRICA

PERSPECTIVES ON AFRICAN BOOK DEVELOPMENT

BOOKS FOR SCHOOLS: IMPROVING ACCESS TO SUPPLEMENTARY READING MATERIALS IN AFRICA

With case studies by:

Wanda do Amaral

Anne Hewling

Cephas Odini

Thuli Radebe

Diana Rosenberg

Amadou Békaye Sidibé

EDITED BY DIANA ROSENBERG

WORKING GROUP
ON BOOKS AND LEARNING MATERIALS
ASSOCIATION FOR THE DEVELOPMENT OF EDUCATION IN AFRICA

Published by the Working Group on Books and Learning Materials
of the Association for the Development of Education in Africa
c/o DFID Education Dept., 94 Victoria St., London SW1E 5JL, United Kingdom

First published 2000

ISBN 1 901830 09 8

Distributed by ABC, African Books Collective Ltd.,
The Jam Factory, 27 Park End Street, Oxford OX1 1HU, United Kingdom
Tel: +44-(0) 1865-726686
Fax: +44-(0) 1865-793298
Email: abc@dial.pipex.com

Packaged by Aldridge Press
24 Thorney Hedge Road, London W4 5SD
Editorial: Cathy Ferreira
Design: Geoffrey Wadsley
Typeset in Trump Medieval, Lithos, Futura, Artefact

Printed and bound in Great Britain by Redwood Books Ltd.
Trowbridge, Wiltshire

CONTENTS

Contents

ACKNOWLEDGEMENTS

The Department for International Development (DFID) provided funding for both the research and the publication of this book. The Association for the Development of Education in Africa (ADEA), through its Working Group on Books and Learning Materials, also contributed towards the costs of publication. An earlier version was published by DFID in June 1998 under the title *Getting Books to School Pupils in Africa*, number 26 in its Education Research series.

Thanks go to Carew Treffgarne, Senior Education Adviser, DFID and Leader of ADEA's Working Group on Books and Learning Materials and Carol Priestley, Coordinator of the Group, for encouraging the idea of research in this area and supporting the long process from research to book.

Thanks also go to Tony Berrett, who translated the Mali case study from French into English and Carol Haddrill, who translated the one from Mozambique from the Portuguese.

To my fellow authors, I owe a great debt. They took up the challenge of writing the case studies with great enthusiasm, overcame difficulties in the field, met the agreed deadlines and patiently answered all my queries.

Diana Rosenberg
March 2000

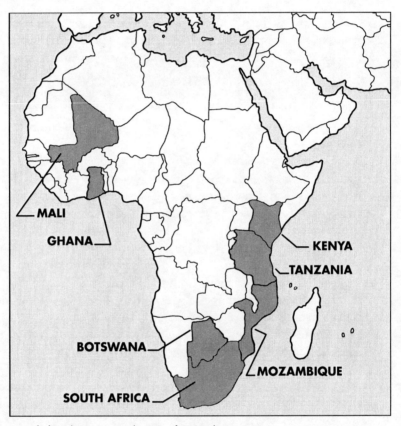

Map of Africa showing country locations of case studies

LIST OF AUTHORS

EDITOR, AUTHOR AND WORKSHOP FACILITATOR:
Diana Rosenberg
Adviser on Books and Libraries, Bristol, UK

AUTHORS OF CASE STUDIES:
Wanda do Amaral
Technical Adviser, Fundo Bibliográfico de Língua Portuguesa,
Maputo, Mozambique

Anne Hewling
J and B Educational, Gaborone, Botswana

Cephas Odini
Dean, Faculty of Information Sciences, Moi University, Eldoret,
Kenya

Thuli Radebe
Director, Research and Knowledge Management, Department of
Public Service and Administration, Pretoria, South Africa
Previously (and at the time of the research) Senior Lecturer,
Information Studies Department, University of Natal, South
Africa

Amadou Békaye Sidibé
Bibliographer, École Nationale d'Administration, Bamako, Mali

LIST OF ABBREVIATIONS AND ACRONYMS

ACCT   Agence de Coopération Culturelle et Technique
ANC   African National Congress (South Africa)
ASBAD   Association Sénégalaise des Bibliothécaires, Archivistes et
         Documentalistes

BAI   Book Aid International
BIEF   Banque Internationale d'Information sur les Etats Francophones (ACCT)
BLD   Bibliothèque–Lecture–Développement (Libraries–Reading–Development)
         (Senegal)
BNLS   Botswana National Library Service
BSU   Bibliothèques Scolaires et Universitaires (a book donation programme
         operating in Mali)

CAP   Educational Support Commission (Mozambique)
CBP   Children's Book Project (Tanzania)
CEPD   Committee for Education Policy Document (South Africa)
CHICSI   Council of Children's Science Publications in Africa
CODE   Canadian Organization for Development through Education
CSS   Central Statistical Services (South Africa)

DEO   District Education Officer (Kenya)
DET   Department of Education and Training (South Africa)
DFID   Department For International Development (UK) (previously known as
         ODA)
DNFE   Department of Non-formal Education (Botswana)
DoE   Department of Education (South Africa)
DSE   German Foundation for International Development

FRELIMO   Front for the Liberation of Mozambique

GDP   Gross domestic product
GLB   Ghana Library Board
GNP   Gross national product

HOA   House of Assembly (South Africa)
HOD   House of Delegates (South Africa)
HOR   House of Representatives (South Africa)

IFLA   International Federation of Library Associations and Institutions
INSET   In-service training
IPET   Implementation Plan for Education and Training (South Africa)
ITEC   Institute of Training and Education for Capacity-Building (South Africa)

JPL	La Joie par les Livres
KIE	Kenya Institute of Education
LAM	Lycée Askia Mohammed (Bamako, Mali)
LIS	Library and information services
LRC	Learning Resource Centre (Kenya)
MINED	Ministry of Education (Mozambique)
NDP	National Development Plan (Botswana)
NEPI	National Education Policy Investigation (South Africa)
NGO	Non-governmental organization
OBE	Outcomes-based education
ODA	Overseas Development Administration (UK) (now known as DFID)
OLP	Opération Lecture Publique (Popular Reading Programme, Mali)
PACEB	Projet d'Appui Canadien à l'Enseignement de Base (Burkina Faso)
PDRH	Programme de Développement des Ressources Humaines (Senegal)
PLIS	Provincial Libraries and Information Service (Eastern Cape, S. A.)
PRESET	Pre-service training
RNPE	Revised National Policy on Education (Botswana)
S.A.	South Africa
SABAP	South African Book Aid Project
SCD	Schools and Colleges Department (of GLB, Ghana)
SELP	Secondary English Language Project (Kenya)
SIAPAC-Africa	Social Impact Assessment and Policy Analysis Corporation (Pty) Ltd. (Botswana)
SLS	School Library Service
SNE	National System of Education (Mozambique)
TAC	Teachers Advisory Centre (Kenya)
TLS	Tanzania Library Services
TRC	Teachers Resource Centre
UK	United Kingdom of Great Britain and Northern Ireland
UNDP	United Nations Development Programme
UNESCO	United Nations Educational, Scientific and Cultural Organization
UNICEF	United Nations Children's Fund
VRR	Village Reading Room (Botswana)
VSO	Voluntary Service Overseas (UK)
ZIP	Zone of Educational Influence (Mozambique)

Chapter One

THE RESEARCH: RATIONALE, METHODOLOGY, LIMITATIONS
DIANA ROSENBERG

> Leaders in the developing countries generally understand the impor-
> tance of investing in basic education. They recognize that high
> levels of literacy and numeracy are prerequisites for creating a
> competitive workforce and a nation of effective parents and active
> citizens. (International Consultative Forum on Education for All,
> 1998:5)

Yet education in Africa is and has been since the 1980s in crisis.
Despite the substantial expansion that occurred in all countries in
the years following independence, there are now stagnating enrolments (although the population continues to increase) and an
overall erosion of quality. Confidence in education as a way
towards development no longer exists as strongly as it did before
(Sturges and Neill, 1998:155).

Many studies have been undertaken and conclusions reached on
the best ways to revitalize education in Africa. The key is thought
to be in the restoration of an efficient mix of inputs and depends on
correcting the imbalance between salary and non-salary expenditures, such as teacher training, buildings and instructional materials. Shortage of good quality learning materials remains the main
stumbling block to literacy and effective schooling. In 1983 educational materials accounted for just 1.1% of the recurrent primary
education budget (taking the median for all African countries), i.e.
less than US$0.60 per pupil per year. The comparable figure for
developed countries is 4%, i.e. US$100 per pupil per year (World
Bank, 1988:35). The same World Bank report maintained that:

> ... there is strong evidence that increasing the provision of instruc-
> tional materials, especially textbooks, is the most cost-effective way
> of raising the quality of primary education. The scarcity of learning
> materials in the classroom is the most serious impediment to
> educational effectiveness in Africa. It is certainly here that the gap
> in educational provision between this region and the rest of the
> world has grown widest. (World Bank, 1988:42)

And the same is true for all levels of education.

Providing an adequate supply of relevant and appropriate reading and other instructional and learning materials for use by teachers and their pupils is not just a question of money for purchase. Such provision entails the authorship, publication and printing of the materials, together with availability of raw materials, like paper. Also essential to the process is their distribution into the hands of the users, either directly or indirectly, via storage, organization, control and dissemination by an information centre or library. 'There are three basic ways to obtain a book – buy, borrow or receive as a gift' (Smith, 1978). In Africa, the major constraint on book buying is poverty. Whereas course textbooks can be distributed through retail outlets and individual purchase, reference and general reading materials require some form of organization for shared use. Books are too expensive for any but those which are compulsory reading to be purchased. It is not feasible to expect an individual to buy a book for reference or for once-only reading.

The importance of *school libraries*, the final element in the book chain, has not gone unrecognized. Book sector studies, from the 1980s onwards, have been undertaken in many countries in Africa and libraries were included in the overall analysis. Another World Bank report (Fuller, 1986) noted that school libraries are one of the investments that influence the quality of schooling to a great extent. Fifteen out of eighteen studies undertaken by the World Bank covering the intensity of use of school libraries, indicated that they contribute to a pupil's high achievement in school work. Yet such *traditional* school libraries are expensive and involve both investing in buildings, facilities, stock acquisition and training, as well as establishing adequate recurrent budgets to maintain the system created. What has been neglected is the development of cost reduction strategies, so that delivery mechanisms are consistent with local conditions and requirements. Providing access to learning resources need not necessarily be through the traditional western model of 'one school, one library'. There are other options and alternatives which will still put learning resources into the hands of school learners, so as to ensure that pupils can and do read.

It is the aim of this study to examine some of the models through which the school population in Africa gain access to supplementary reading materials and to reach some conclusions on which are the most efficient and effective.

Supplementary reading

Definition and role

Textbooks are written to support a specific course and relate directly to the syllabus of that course. Supplementary books include non-fiction reference and general books which supplement course textbooks by offering alternative approaches, additional information and knowledge of subjects not directly covered by the school curriculum, as well as fiction including story books, poetry, and drama. The importance to the educational process of access to a wide variety of reading materials is widely recognized. Vincent Greaney prefaced the collection of articles he edited on the promotion of reading in developing countries (1996:1) with the statement:

> Arguably, the most important element of a quality education program is literacy. Without the ability to read, people are denied access to pertinent information about health, social, cultural and political issues as well as sources of pleasure and enrichment. For a population to become literate, it must have access to a supply of relevant and enlivening textbooks and supplementary reading material. Young people especially need access to high-quality books to develop not only the ability to read but also the reading habit.

An information-rich environment encourages innovation and creative ideas to flourish. Without the opportunity to read widely, what is taught in the classroom is not reinforced and the quality and permanence of the benefits of education are endangered. Without it, students cannot develop skills of locating, selecting, organizing, manipulating, analyzing, evaluating and presenting information. Without it, the education process fails to develop beyond the acquisition of the most basic knowledge and becomes the mechanical acquisition of factual information prescribed by a syllabus and examination board. Broad reading of self-selected material is associated with the acquisition of vocabulary and comprehension skills and the development of the reading habit and the creative imagination. Reading skills lie at the heart of effective learning in all subject areas. In short, access to supplementary reading materials:

- develops the ability to read, write and comprehend and extends the vocabulary;
- develops a teaching force which is capable of moving beyond the confines of set books and textbooks;
- supplements and enriches work done by pupils in the classroom;
- encourages independent access to information and arouses the interest of pupils in matters outside the curriculum;
- develops the reading habit and encourages the growth of the creative imagination;

3

- provides training and experience in the use and retrieval of information, a skill which is essential for problem solving, higher education and lifelong learning.

Strategies and impact

The argument, that the supply of supplementary reading materials (or the promotion of wide or extensive reading programmes which rely on the availability of those materials) relates to achievement of high levels of literacy, has been won time and again. A review of the evidence now available on whether literature-based instruction and wide reading actually have a positive influence on children's growth as readers has been made by Anderson (1996). He concludes that reading may be about ten times more important as a source of vocabulary growth than direct vocabulary instruction and that the amount of reading undertaken is consistently associated with reading proficiency and topical knowledge. An increase in the amount of children's playful, stimulating experience with good books leads to accelerated growth in reading competence. And this conclusion holds true whether for English-speaking children learning to read English, or for children from various language groups learning their home language or a second language from their own country or a foreign language. It also holds true at all levels of education. Effective learning cannot take place without effective reading and reading is the foundation for all subjects taught at primary and secondary level. '... once pupils have learned "how to read" they can only develop the skill by reading. Good readers read a lot, and pupils therefore need to be given the opportunity to read' (Williams, 1998:65).

Book floods are one strategy that has been used to increase the amount of reading material available. Students are immersed in high-interest books designed to be read, discussed and shared in various ways. Examples from the developing world come from Fiji, Singapore and Sri Lanka (Elley, 1996; Sri Lanka, 1996). Evidence shows that book floods bring dramatic improvements in reading, writing, listening, vocabulary and grammar, especially for younger age groups and where children are learning in a language different from their home language. The Sri Lanka pilot project provided between 100 and 200 books per school, for Years 4 and 5. Those in the project schools gained three times as much in reading as those in the control schools, together with parallel improvements in writing and listening comprehension. Positive changes were also noticed in pupils' attitudes towards reading as a valuable resource for learning. Situations in these countries are very similar to those in Africa.

A different approach to the instructional process has been tried out in Latin America. In the *Nueva Escuela* of Colombia and the *Nueva Escuela Unitaria* of Guatemala, textbooks have been replaced by self-instructional study guides, supplemented by a rich array of supplementary reading and reference materials (Colbert, Chiappe and Arboleda, 199?; Kraft, 1998; McEwan, 1995; Psacharopoulos, Rojas and Velez, 1989; Rodríguez-Trujillo, 1996). Results are good, in that students from these schools score higher in most cognitive and non-cognitive tests.

However, whether or not textbooks should be replaced by supplementary reading materials remains in contention. Providing non-textbook materials can be a difficult task for many developing countries, because of their limited publishing capacity. In such a situation, it is argued that textbooks remain a viable solution, so long as they are complemented by other materials (Oliveira, 1996). An alternative suggestion is that textbooks in content areas (e.g. mathematics, science, social studies) should be introduced only after children have developed competence and confidence in their reading and writing, i.e. after having been exposed to a variety of books (Elley, 1996:161).

Delivery models

The importance to the education process in developing countries of a supply of supplementary reading materials may well have been accepted. However, in depth discussion on the ways and means through which school pupils access these materials, that is the models of delivery, has failed to take place. Once suitable reading and instructional materials have been written, published, printed and distributed, there needs to be a support structure to regulate their organization and use. That is obvious and school libraries are seen as the answer to putting learning resources into the hands of learners. But school libraries can take many forms. It is this that tends to be overlooked by educational planners. The *traditional* school library evolved and gained acceptance as a delivery system in the West. But is it the most desirable and suitable model for the economic, social and cultural conditions of Africa? Are there alternative models which might also provide learners with access to library-based resources?

Traditional school libraries

The establishment of traditional school libraries – the 'one school, one library' model – has always been the preferred solution to providing access to supplementary reading material. It is considered to most effectively implement the principles laid down in the

UNESCO/IFLA (International Federation of Library Associations and Institutions) School Library Manifesto (1998) and is the model adopted in most Western countries, including the UK (Kinnell, 1992) and the USA.

In Africa, too, the 'one school, one library' model has been favoured. Librarians themselves have been fervent and articulate advocates. A recurrent theme of school library literature in the 1980s and 1990s was the necessity to look for innovative solutions to the inadequate state of school libraries in Africa. IFLA decided to examine the problem in a pre-session seminar in 1993; its aim was to examine the philosophy and operation of school libraries and look for ways to motivate authorities and agencies (Johnson, 1995). In 1995 a seminar in Uganda was held to generate interest in the establishment of school libraries (Abidi, 1996). Mali is an example of a country which has recently and for the first time established a school library programme at the basic level. Tanzania now has a similar policy.

Features of the *traditional* school library are:
- it has a central location from which the library and information service is delivered to the school;
- the service is operated by a professional librarian trained in the provision, organization, management and utilization of resources and information;
- it has purpose built or designed accommodation, furniture and equipment.

Its main functions are:
- to acquire and provide access to learning materials that complement, enrich and support the curriculum;
- to promote their use;
- to provide links to the wider library and information network;
- to encourage the development of information skills;
- to encourage reading for enjoyment.

Alternative models

The *traditional* school library model has not had notable success, even in the West. In the UK, the policy laid down in the 1940s and 1950s that every secondary school should have its own library was never fulfilled; nor was the school library resource centre of the 1970s any more successful. School libraries are seen as being underfunded and underused. In the USA, there seems to be confusion over the role of school libraries and a gap between the views of users and librarians (Feather and Sturges, 1996). Certainly the growth and development of school libraries has not matched those in higher education.

In Africa (and developing countries in general), whilst the need for education has been recognized, the need for school libraries has not. Governments and Ministries of Education have not accepted that library and book provision should be a component of educational investment. The establishment and maintenance of school libraries has been relegated to the last place on the scale of priorities. The majority of schools possess no library. Where some semblance of a school library does exist, it is often no more than a few shelves of outdated and worn out material, inadequately staffed and thus marginal to the teaching-learning process.

In recent years there have been some initiatives in Africa aimed at improving the availability of reading materials in schools, without actually re-establishing school libraries in their traditional form. The rationale for this trend is illustrated by the debate that is taking place in South Africa (Bawa, 1993; Karlsson, 1996). Whilst it is recognized that the provision of relevant resources to basic education learners is a state responsibility, lack of finance makes the prospect of providing every school with a library a pipe-dream. Costs and standards of this model are unrealistically high and unattainable at the moment. The state is compelled to prioritize in directions other than school libraries; if a school cannot afford basic textbooks and teachers and classrooms, it cannot afford a library. It is therefore necessary for those involved in the provision of learning resources to 'do more with less' and to consider the alternatives to the traditional Western model of one school, one library. This necessity can also be viewed as an opportunity; the alternatives may prove more appropriate to the new education philosophy that is being evolved and may offer ways of better integrating delivery models with the needs of curriculum and classroom practices. If this is true of South Africa, a country with one of the highest gross national products in Africa, then the one school, one library model is going to be even less attainable for other countries on the continent.

The discussion document prepared in South Africa by the Centre for Educational Technology and Distance Education (1997) identifies seven possible school library models:

- one school, one library (the traditional school library already discussed above);
- one classroom, one library;
- one cluster, one library (where a number of schools share one library);
- one community, one library (libraries which are shared between school learners, teachers and the general public);
- one region, one library service (where a regional library service provides library-related services to schools within a region, ranging from advice and training to supply of

materials; usually called a school library service);

- one learner, one library (learners have electronic access to resources located beyond the confines of the school);
- one lifelong learner, one library (caters for the needs of a wide range of learners at different ages or educational levels; often an integral part of community learning centres or educational development centres).

Each model provides library-based resources to educators and learners. However, each is different in terms of the size, nature and development of the collection, human resourcing, management, funding and mode of service delivery. Divisions between the models are not necessarily watertight and within each model there may be different modes of delivery. For example, book boxes might be supplied to schools under the one classroom, one library model, the one cluster, one library model or the one region, one library model. A school with a library might also be supported by a regional library service.

Examples of alternative models can now be found throughout Africa. One is that of community resource centres, which aim to provide reference and referral services to the whole community. These centres are often located in schools and tend to be mostly used by school children and their teachers. Notable examples are found in the rural areas of Botswana and Zimbabwe; Ghana has its Community Libraries Project; they also exist in most other African countries. Another is the establishment of teachers' resource centres, now found throughout Africa, e.g. Eritrea, Kenya, Namibia, Uganda, Zambia. They are set up to serve a number of schools and stock a variety of teacher and pupil textbooks, reference books and sets of books for use in the classroom. There has been a resurgence of interest in the use of classroom libraries and book box libraries; examples are found in Mozambique, Namibia and South Africa. South Africa has a pilot project involving the establishment of Learning and Education Centres and is experimenting with virtual libraries through the School Net project. Increasingly non-governmental organizations (NGOs), rather than government, are providing support in the provision of reading materials; there is the Ghana Book Trust; READ in South Africa is well known; BLD (Bibliothèque-Lecture-Développement – Libraries-Reading-Development) is a recent arrival in Senegal.

Case studies

There is therefore a proliferation of access or delivery models now in existence across Africa. But little research has yet been carried out into their operation and use. This study was therefore set up with the objective of understanding which work best and in which circumstances, and to recommend what strategy or strategies are affordable and sustainable. Given the lack of published data, it was decided that a case study approach was the most feasible and practical. By examining and evaluating in depth a different model in a different country, it is hoped that the resulting information will provide some indication of how successful (or otherwise) the various models are in providing access to supplementary reading materials and point the way for further research.

Available finance limited the case studies to six:
- school library services (Ghana, Tanzania)
- school libraries (Mali)
- classroom libraries, NGO-supported (South Africa)
- book box libraries (Mozambique)
- teachers' resource centres (Kenya)
- community resource centres (Botswana)

Nationals, employed in the information field and with a record of research and interest in school level information provision, were recruited to undertake the case studies in Botswana, Kenya, Mali, Mozambique and South Africa. The case study on school library services (mainly of historical significance) was to be undertaken from an examination of the published literature.

Preliminary workshop

Before the local researchers started their case study research, a workshop was held in London in September 1997. The purpose was to establish a common approach and methodology, so that all the case studies would be undertaken along the same lines and the resulting data would be comparable. Specifically the aims of the workshop were:
- to discuss and identify the factors that determine information provision and delivery, in the context of library-based resources at the school level;
- to explore and discuss concepts and methods of evaluation and their appropriateness for assessing the performance and impact of different models of delivery and access;
- to provide researchers with the opportunity to develop, present and discuss their research strategies;
- to develop and agree:
  - a common methodological framework on which to base each case study;
  - a timetable for completion;

– details of data presentation.

One day was spent on issues in case study strategy, including objectives of providing access, factors in providing access, ways of analysis, ways of evaluation, types of data and methods of data collection. Researchers then prepared and presented a research strategy for their particular case study. Finally a common framework and timetable for the case studies was agreed and common data collection instruments designed.

It was agreed that each case study would be submitted by the end of December 1997 and would cover the topics listed below:

- **country context:** socio-economic situation; educational policies and practices; information provision strategies in general and in particular at the school level;
- **background of model:** stakeholders / objectives / critical success factors; origins, history, development; functions; governance; target user populations;
- **methodology:** choice and rationale; methods used in data collection and analysis; sample; problems;
- **analysis:** collection development; staffing; physical facilities; finance; use;
- **evaluation:** measures of cost, effectiveness and user satisfaction; assessment of effectiveness; impact;
- **conclusions:** overall assessment; future prospects; future strategies.

Problems and limitations

The overall methodology of this research, based as it is on the labour of local researchers working in relative isolation, inevitably resulted in case studies which vary greatly in depth and quality. The findings are not easily comparable. Although the preliminary workshop went some way towards lessening this limitation by providing a common framework and designing common data collection instruments, greater consistency could only have been achieved through much closer co-operation and co-ordination in both data collection and data analysis. Once the case studies had been submitted, it was not feasible to request any further data collection. One case study – that of community resource centres in Botswana – was not completed during the first phase of the research.

Local researchers met with time and funding constraints. Two months maximum was allowed for planning and gaining authority for the research, as well as collecting the data. Funding was restricted to covering stationery and a small amount of travel. Researchers had to fit in the research with their normal work load.

Data collection had to be limited to small and local samples; for example, the researcher in South Africa could only sample three districts in the Pietermaritzburg area. In Mozambique, neither time nor the available budget allowed travel to Cabo Delgado, the location of one of the projects examined, in the far north of the country. And these constraints were sometimes exacerbated by events in-country. In Kenya the teachers went on strike; there was little time left for data collection when they returned and it was therefore restricted to only one district (instead of the two planned) and to Teachers Advisory Centres at the primary level. In South Africa, the data collection time coincided with school examinations; therefore not a lot of time could be expected from the teachers. In Mozambique the schools were closed in December and January, another reason why data collection could not be extended to Cabo Delgado. Mali suffered from student strikes, which resulted in the closure of schools during October and November.

All researchers met with a lack of existing hard data, in particular statistics of cost and use. The intention had been to rely as much as possible on published (for example annual reports) and unpublished sources (such as records of income and expenditure, of purchase, of stock, of loans and visits) and to concentrate on finding out about user satisfaction and perceived impact of the delivery model during any interviews. But such records had not been maintained. In the school library services case study, where it had been hoped to rely on the journal articles and books already published, it was found that information was only available for the period of first establishment, with nothing on the succeeding years. (Local researchers were then employed to gather data, but even so operational details were hard to come by, particularly in relation to costs.) In Kenya, those in charge of Teachers Advisory Centres did not maintain records on the use or size of collections. In Mozambique, the complete archive documenting the mobile book box libraries had been destroyed. All case studies therefore suffer from incomplete data, especially where costs are concerned.

The intention had been to cover the provision of educational materials at both the primary and secondary level. In the event, four of the case studies are restricted to the primary level: book boxes, classroom libraries, teachers' advisory centres and community resource centres. (In Kenya, it had been planned to also study the very similar learning resource centres that operate at the secondary level, but time did not allow.) Only that of Mali examined school libraries at both levels, whilst the school library services of Ghana and Tanzania only served secondary schools. Although the Mali study concluded that the problems facing school libraries were much the same at both levels and one of the recommendations from teachers interviewed in South Africa was that the classroom library programme be extended to secondary schools, the level of education addressed by each model must be born in mind when general conclusions are reached. Some, but not necessarily all, will be applicable to both levels of education.

During the preliminary workshop, it was agreed that the assessment of the various models would be through measures of effectiveness, whether of their performance or their impact on the education process as a whole. Effectiveness assessment within the context of defined educational objectives and learner outcomes provides a strong argument for the value of programmes, this being the kind of information that decision makers want when they ask for accountability. They have to be convinced that libraries and librarians make a clear and valuable impact on student learning and the overall performance goals of the school. A school administrator prioritizes the allocation of resources to the programmes that are most effective in terms of student outcomes. Attempts were therefore made to gather information on the size, sufficiency, relevance and costs of collections, their services and the use made of them. For impact, changes were sought in areas like pupil abilities and examination pass rates.

However this approach does have integral problems (Berkowitz, 1994). There is no agreement on the definition of effectiveness nor techniques for its measurement in the information field. An accepted measure of what constitutes effective provision is lacking. It is simple enough to collect data on collection size or the number of loans; it is much more difficult to decide on measures that show the effects of a library's performance on student success and on the type of data that needs to be gathered. It seems far easier to identify problems that inhibit success than to identify elements that enable successful programme implementation. Satisfaction with a service is not an absolute but depends on prior expectations. A teacher or a pupil who has not previously been exposed to any book provision, is likely to be pleased to receive anything and therefore express satisfaction. Impact is also a particularly elusive concept. In education, it is difficult to link an outcome to a particular input, such as provision of books. Various other factors such as teachers, buildings and facilities like equipment have also to be considered. One has to rely on perceptions rather than actual cause-to-effect evidence.

Using any form of cost-benefit or cost-effectiveness analysis proved even more problematic. These methodologies were discussed during the workshop and it was agreed that it might be feasible to examine the cost-effectiveness of a model by developing cost indicators and then weighing these against the efficiency and effectiveness of the service. Such indicators could be the cost per item or the cost per pupil per year. However, this form of analysis is very demanding in terms of data requirements. It could only be used if the cost data was already available; in the event very little cost data was obtained by researchers.

Review and revision

A report was submitted to the Department for International Development, UK, (DFID) in April 1998 and published as a paper in its *Education Research* series (Rosenberg, 1998). A small group of experts was called together to discuss the report. It was felt that, given the paucity of published work concerning different models of school library delivery in Africa and the problems facing governments in this area, particularly at a time when education in Africa is becomingly increasingly resource-based and is changing from rote to process learning, the report might be adapted for publication in the *Perspectives on African Books Development* series by the Association for the Develpment of Education in Africa (ADEA).

In particular, it was recommended that:

- the case study on community resource centres be re-commissioned, so that evidence from this model could be included and compared with other models;
- a new chapter giving an overview of the development of school book provision in all countries in Africa be included;
- the conclusion is not restricted to evidence from the case studies, but addresses issues in general and uses data arising from other research in the same subject area.

A chapter covering the history and development of school book provision in Africa and its determining factors therefore follows. Then come six chapters, each one devoted to a case study of one model of access from one country in Africa. The final chapter discusses the issues involved in library provision and attempts to reach some conclusions as to which model might be most effective and cost effective. More details about the individual methodologies used for each case study are included in the relevant chapter and any data collecting instruments used can be found in the Appendix. A bibliography, including references cited in the text, completes the book.

Chapter Two

THE CONTEXT: HISTORY AND DEVELOPMENT OF LIBRARY PROVISION IN AFRICAN SCHOOLS
DIANA ROSENBERG

School libraries of all types have a long history, but in most countries of the world their development has been neglected. A recent survey (Johnson, 1995) produced information about school libraries in 64 countries. Provision varied but, in general, school libraries were marginalized and were not seen as high priority.

In Africa, school libraries are the poor of a library world not over-abundant in riches (Olden, 1995:127; Sturges and Neill, 1998:153). If they exist at all, they are inadequately staffed, amount to no more than shelves of out-dated and worn out material and are marginal in terms of impact on the teaching/learning process. The importance of school libraries has not been recognized as an integral part of educational planning.

The development of school library programmes in post-Independence Africa falls into three distinct phases, albeit with differences between countries and regions:
- strengthening and expansion, ending in the 1970s;
- the lost decades, until the end of the 1980s and extending in some cases to date;
- growth of project-dependent services, from the beginning of the 1990s.

Strengthening and expansion

During the 19th and early 20th century, with the exception of Ethiopia, Liberia and South Africa, the African continent had been divided up into the protectorates and colonies of European nations, in particular France, Great Britain and Portugal. When Independence was achieved, mainly during the late 1950s and early 1960s, patterns of library development, including school libraries, mirrored the colonial model. For school libraries, both public and private, this meant centralized library collections at secondary level, with centralized and/or class collections at primary level.

However these school collections were far from satisfactory, as various surveys undertaken immediately after Independence indicate:

- **Botswana** According to the new Director of the public library service writing in 1966, school and college libraries

  > were poorly equipped and furnished, stocked with unattractive and haphazard collections, shabby second-hand gifts of books, staffed, if at all, by a succession of voluntary or part-time workers with little or no library training and little or no money with which to maintain their libraries in good condition. (Baffour-Awuah, 1998)

- **East Africa** In his 1960 report on the development of library services in East Africa, Hockey summed up his visits to 75 mainly secondary level schools as a 'most depressing experience'. The book stock was inadequate and unsuitable, the accommodation poor. Consequently, the teachers were uninterested.

- **Ghana** It was not until 1970 that a committee was given the assignment of investigating the position of secondary school and teacher training college libraries. The report found that accommodation was poor, with 85% of the institutions housing libraries in small single rooms. Book stocks were grossly inadequate and, in some schools, locked away in cupboards. Budgets were static and there was a lack of proper organization stemming from the lack of trained library staff. Furniture was generally of poor quality and inappropriate. In general library provision was haphazard and depended entirely on the interest and enthusiasm of the individual headmaster or principal (Ofori, 1981).

- **Namibia** At Independence in 1990, less than 23% of Namibian schools had a book collection. Only between 16.4% and 19.2% of school pupils had been exposed to library books and only 26.5% of Namibian teachers had access to a book collection. Within these figures there was a bias towards the old-white schools. The 66 old-white schools had 71% of school library books; the remaining 1,087 schools shared 29% of the remaining books, with the far north of Namibia having less than 1%. If the former white schools were excluded, the average number of books per pupil was 0.3 (Tötemeyer, 1993).

- **Tanzania** Research on school libraries, undertaken from 1968 to 1970, showed that:

  > In secondary schools, head teachers received a grant to cover all expenditures and that the amount spent on the library was at the discretion of the head teacher and largely dependent on

other financial exigencies. Primary schools received no specific grant for school libraries and were dependent on donations or on raising money locally. In terms of numbers, the book stock position in secondary schools was unsatisfactory and in terms of quality the books were out of date. The organization of the library was unsatisfactory and normally in the hands of an already overworked teacher who was usually not qualified for library work. Very few schools had purposely built libraries and their equipment and furniture were unsuitable for library use. Finally, the school library was not well used and, if at all, it was used as a study area especially for senior pupils. (Kaungamno, 1981)

In Anglophone Africa, the answer to this gloomy state of school library provision was seen to be the establishment of school library support services, either as an arm of the public library services or as an integral part of the Ministry of Education and either at national or provincial/state level. Such a service could both upgrade existing libraries and encourage the establishment of new ones by offering advice in their management, by training staff, by topping-up of collections, by aiding the selection, purchase and processing of book stock.

The continent already had an example of school library services successfully operated through a Ministry of Education. In South Africa, in the post-war period, a decision had been taken that a school library service was different in kind from other library services, having no rationale in terms of its operational procedure other than that of being an instrument of formal education. Education (for whites) was organized on a provincial basis, the Transvaal Education Department Library Services, inaugurated in 1951, is an example of a school library service. Centralized libraries within each school were essential and schools were given generous allocations to purchase library materials. The Library Services headquarters provided a display and lists of recommended books, plus a repair and rebinding scheme. It provided refresher courses for school librarians and guidance in introduction of courses in the use of books and libraries. Advisers visited each school regularly. Centralized cataloguing was also introduced. Similar services for Asian, coloured and black communities were operated at national level, though with lower levels of funding.

In the countries of Anglophone Africa that achieved Independence in the 1950s and '60s, the new national public library services took the responsibility for organizing school library services, sometimes in collaboration with or at the request of the Ministry of Education. It was the Hockey report (1960, on which much national library service legislation was based) that encouraged this approach. Hockey saw the national library service to be the natural home of a school library service, because of:

- the need to co-ordinate school libraries with the development of teacher training college libraries;
- the necessity of co-ordinating school libraries with the development of a public library service for children run by the library board;
- the inadequacy of school libraries arising out of the lack of books;
- the uncritical acceptance of gifts of books and the need to train teachers in the basic principles of the selection of books for schools;
- the absolute necessity of widening the horizons of students and teachers beyond the confines of set books and school textbooks (Kaungamno, 1981:108).

In Ghana it was recognized that a healthy level of public library membership depended on people being introduced to the reading habit whilst they were at school, through good school libraries. Ghana Library Board was therefore convinced that it needed to be involved in the development and upgrading of school libraries.

A detailed account of the development of school library services in the two countries of Africa – Ghana and Tanzania – that took the concept farthest, is given in the next chapter. But many other countries, where national or state public library systems were established, also set up school library support services. Examples are:

- **Botswana** The National Library Services Act of 1967 provided for the establishment of an Educational Libraries Division specifically to address educational library needs in the country. Services immediately established were book box services for primary schools and a mobile library service for secondary schools (Baffour-Awuah, 1998).
- **Nigeria** State Library Boards were encouraged to establish school library services. The most effective were in Lagos (which was the home of the UNESCO pilot project for school libraries in Africa), the Mid-West and the South-Eastern States (Kaungamno and Ilomo, 1979:46; Nwoye, 1981).
- **Zambia** One of the objectives of the Zambia National Library Service is 'to run a school library service' (Kalusopa and Chifwepa, 1997).

In many countries, however, school libraries remained the responsibility of individual schools and their development was according to the whims of individual headteachers or class teachers, using the book budget provided by the Ministry of Education. This was true for Francophone Africa, where neither national public library services nor school library support services had developed, and for countries such as Kenya and Uganda, where the public library services did not take up responsibilities for school libraries. The results were haphazard: sometimes a good school library or class collection developed, but there was no guarantee that the same sort of service would be found in schools all over the country. Smaller schemes did evolve, but tended to die an early death. An early example was the attempt of the Ministry of Education in Ghana in 1956 to set up classroom libraries for all primary schools in the country. The operation folded in 1958 (Ofori, 1981). Another was the book box scheme for primary schools developed in 1969 by the Uganda School Library Association and the British Council. It covered a limited number of schools and books were distributed and exchanged each term. It disappeared in the early 1970s (Byaruhanga, 1972). Many national library services also offered book boxes and schools could join such schemes, on payment of the subscription required.

The lost decades

The period from the end of the 1970s until even the present have been called 'the lost decades' of African librarianship, a period when early hopes of continued growth and expansion evaporated and library services of all types decayed and deteriorated. These years have been especially difficult for what was already the Cinderella service. Except in South Africa and some of the nations of Southern Africa, like Botswana, governments failed to provide enough money to support school libraries, either through direct funding to schools or through centralized services. Legislation and policies that existed on the establishment of school libraries were ignored and few more enacted.

Examples of some of the reports that have been made about school library provision in various countries from a variety of sources indicate the general lack of school access to supplementary reading materials that existed and, in many countries, continues to exist.

- **Angola** Until 1982 and the resumption of war, libraries were supported and Luanda in particular had many school libraries. But by 1994, few remained in operation and it would be necessary to re-launch them (Aparicio, 1997).
- **Cameroon** Although a levy is collected from each pupil for library development, it is thought that few collections exist either at primary or secondary level, outside the private sector. Libraries lack buildings, budgets and trained staff (Balock, 1997).

19

- **Ethiopia** The journal *Link-Up* provides many examples submitted by readers of the grim state of school library provision in Ethiopia. Facilities are poor, furniture and equipment lacking, books outdated, budget meagre or nil. One Ethiopian librarian contends that if Ethiopian libraries were measured by the state of the average school library, it could be said that they are non-existent (Dawit, 1998).
- **Gabon** At primary level, libraries barely exist. At secondary level only a minority, generally those administered by religious missions, have a library with a regular budget and qualified personnel (ADG, 1993).
- **Kenya** Addressing the Kenya Library Association in 1989, Mrs Masiga, then Assistant Chief Inspector of Schools, introduced her paper with a quick overview:

  > The surveys done by the inspectors during school inspections reveal an unhappy situation. Most primary schools do not have provision for a library for their pupils at all. Secondary schools are not in a better position either. Most of them are struggling to establish libraries whose stock and maintenance is extremely worrying. At present the position of libraries is not seen as a priority.

- **Nigeria** The 1981 National Policy on Education included mention of libraries with the ringing statement that:

  > Libraries are one of the most important educational services. Every State Ministry needs to provide funds for the establishment of libraries in all our educational institutions and train librarians and library assistants for this service. (Apeji, 1997)

  After 1981 all mention of libraries disappeared from official policy documents (Adekanmbi, 1998). By the 1990s 'libraries were said to be in a deplorable condition in virtually all the public sector schools' and a survey undertaken of secondary schools in one district revealed that although staff in the form of teacher-librarians were mostly present, collections were out of date and small, libraries were usually a collection housed in a classroom, sometimes without shelves, there were no separate budgets and 73% of users considered them inadequate (Adelusi, 1998).
- **Senegal** Following the 1976 law which was to put in place a national system of libraries, a survey was carried out in 1992 to discover what had been done in the sphere of school libraries (Diop and Kabou, 1992). An analysis of the first 66 returns received revealed there was a lack of facilities (only ten had purpose built premises), restricted finance (only five, three private and two public, had budgets), collections which

relied heavily on donation, were numerically insufficient and made up essentially of textbooks and few libraries with trained staff. Corréa, writing in 1997, estimated that in Dakar only 15% of primary schools, 20% of junior secondary schools and 30% of lycées had libraries; in the provinces only 25% of schools had libraries.

- **Tanzania** A 1989 Books Subsector Study (Carpenter and Kemp, 1989) declared the current situation of education libraries in Tanzania to be dismal. Although most secondary schools had purpose built libraries, their role was ill defined, there was no financial provision for the purchase of new materials, the book stocks were mostly donated, inappropriate, in poor repair and out of date, and the teacher-librarians mismatched to the jobs. In primary schools, there were virtually no libraries of any sort at all.

- **Zambia** Carpenter and her colleagues found a similar situation in Zambia in 1990. Secondary school and teacher-training college libraries were 'mainly responsive passive elements', with outdated books showing signs of 'intensive and prolonged use'. In addition there was 'a high proportion of largely irrelevant donated books taking up shelf space which would otherwise be empty' (Carpenter et al., 1990).

  Kalusopa and Chifwepa writing in 1997 confirmed that, although school libraries had been a Zambian government policy since Independence, nothing had so far been achieved. Their survey of secondary school libraries in the Copperbelt found that most schools did not provide any meaningful services. Funding was either non-existent or inadequate, buildings poor with little seating, collections out of date and dependent on donations, only one school had a trained staff, most libraries had no catalogue.

- **Zimbabwe** In 1989 the situation was similar to how it had been at Independence nine years earlier. Most schools had no library. Often the library was merely a locked cupboard, a storeroom with books in a corner or a collection in the head-teacher's office. Teachers did not use the library, neither students nor parents saw any link between libraries and education.

During this period of 'the lost decades', neither governments nor educators expressed more than a vague interest in the ways and means of providing supplementary reading materials in schools. Nevertheless, a feature of this period is that librarians, particularly those from countries where services had started to develop and then wither, campaigned vigorously on two fronts for the establishment of a legally backed government policy to require schools to establish libraries and the setting up of centralized support services; and for the establishment of stated standards to govern the development of school libraries:

- **Ghana** Alemna in 1993 saw it as essential that the standards embodied in *A Manual for School Libraries in Ghana* published in 1972 be updated and made more relevant to local conditions.

- **Kenya** The Librarian of the Kenya Institute of Education (Mulaha, 1983) recommended that the Ministry of Education should develop guidelines and a school library service to support them; also that there must be an Inspectorate to ensure the smooth running of the libraries and the network. It was the holding of the International Federation of Library Associations and Institutions (IFLA) conference in Nairobi in 1984 (Musisi, 1993) that gave impetus to the Kenya Library Association and the Kenya National Library Services to join hands in consolidating the existing government policies on the provision of libraries in secondary schools (Mulaha, 1986:26). The *Guidelines* (Kenya Library Association, 1986) covered acceptable levels for buildings, equipment, books, staff, training, costs and management of libraries in primary, secondary and college libraries.

- **Nambia** From Independence onwards, librarians brought what pressure they could on the government for legislation incorporating the setting up of libraries in every school and college (Tötemeyer, 1996).

- **Senegal** At the initiative of professional librarians a seminar was held under the aegis of the Ministry of National Education to discuss and establish a national policy for school libraries (Politique nationale des bibliothèques scolaires au Sénégal, 1994).

- **Tanzania** Although the Tanzania Library Services Board Act of 1975 included school library provision, attempts were made during the 1980s to strengthen this law. In 1986 *School Library Resource Centre Regulations* were passed, followed a year later by *Standards and Manual for School and College Librarians in Tanzania*, published by Tanzania Library Services (Carpenter and Kemp, 1989).

- **Uganda** A UNESCO mission in 1978 recommended the establishment of a Department of School Libraries in the Ministry of Education and the setting up of a model library as a pilot project (Songa, 1996), but it was not until 1995 that librarians took part in a seminar to design an official school library policy (Abidi, 1996). This was based on setting up a library in every school and included some standards on size of collection, methods of funding, etc.

However, nothing concrete in the way of implementation or the improvement of school library provision resulted from these initiatives.

Project-dependent services

The 1990s have seen new types of school library services develop, ones that are outside of and largely independent of the previous government controlled operations. Although each differs from the other, characteristics are:

- they are established as projects in a partnership between government and foreign aid organizations, assisted by local NGOs; most of the funding comes from overseas agencies;
- they may be projects which are solely directed towards school library provision or projects in which library provision is part of wider educational objectives;
- they can be in support of centralized school library development or supply supplementary reading materials through alternative models.

It is in Francophone West Africa, where little input was made to school libraries in the years after Independence, that projects are found in most countries and projects concerned solely with book provision to schools. Those found in Mali are discussed in depth in the case study in Chapter Four. Others are:

- **Benin** Here Opération Lecture Publique (OLP – Popular Reading Programme – a programme set up by the French Ministère de la Coopération – French Co-operation – in many Francophone countries to establish and support libraries) has decided to address the problem of getting books to schools in rural areas. A central library has been equipped with suitable books and staff and a boat delivers book boxes, each containing 50 titles, to schools and collects/replaces them on the next trip (Nardi, 1998).
- **Burkina Faso** A Canadian project offering support to primary education (Projet d'Appui Canadien à l'Enseignment de Base – PACEB) started in 1995, operates a system of book boxes as a strategy to improve the quality of education (Wininga, 1999).
- **Côte d'Ivoire** Projet Ecole 2000 has been established with the assistance of French Co-operation to support primary education, by encouraging the establishment of school libraries. It is based on teaching inspection districts, each of which receives a library of books and circulates book boxes to the schools. Training both of school librarians and

teachers in teaching with books is included in the project (Salzard and Cosson, 1996; Côte d'Ivoire, 1997).

- **Senegal** Here NGOs are leading the way in establishing libraries in schools. Bibliothèque – Lecture – Développement (BLD; Libraries – Reading – Development) was set up in 1994, initially to manage and extend the Pikine project on the outskirts of Dakar. This had two arms, one circuit of libraries for junior secondary schools and one for the general public. It received funding from the Banque Internationale d'Information sur les Etats Francophone, Canadian Organization for Development through Education (CODE), UNESCO and IFLA (Ndiaye, 1996). Now, with the financial help of CODE, a major programme of BLD is to equip libraries in primary and junior secondary schools in disadvantaged suburban areas with furniture, books, supplies and training of librarians and users. It has also helped in the building and setting up of fifteen libraries in lycées. It would like to extend this programme into rural areas (BLD, 1998).

    Another NGO is Aide et Action, which for several years has been establishing school libraries by providing two books for each enrolled pupil (Aide et Action, 1996). Projet du Développement des Resources Humain (PDRH), a World Bank programme, is also active in the school library field in Senegal. It aims to rehabilitate and equip libraries in fifteen lycées and put in place a national network (Diop and Kabou, 1992).

The projects in Anglophone Africa have in many cases arisen out of English-language teaching support programmes, often financed by the British government. Early examples are those in Tanzania, where provision of graded readers was supported with expert advice and in-service training workshops in the use of supplementary reading materials. In Zanzibar, the English Language Improvement Programme had a wider remit. There, sets of library materials were provided to schools in all subjects, not just English, and multiple copy sets of readers for classroom use could be borrowed by teachers. Libraries with both pupils' collections and teachers' collections were made available in District Education Offices and teachers were trained in library awareness and library use (Carpenter and Kemp, 1989). One of the latest examples of such a project is that being piloted currently in the Anglophone provinces of Cameroon (Primary Extension Reading Project, 1998). Financed by the British Council, books are provided in boxes for use as class libraries at upper primary level.

It is such projects that led to the establishment of Teachers Resource Centres in much of Anglophone Africa, with a remit to transfer teaching and learning materials to schools. The Kenyan Teachers Centres are examined in Chapter Seven.

South Africa, through READ (a case study in Chapter Five) provides an example of an NGO taking charge of book provision to schools. Another more recent South African project is the South Africa Book Aid Project (SABAP). Financed by the British Department for International Development (DFID), one of its objectives is to improve access to books in primary schools. Three regions are participating. In the first to start in the Eastern Cape, District Education Resource Centres were used to send on bags of books to schools, on a rotating basis. Training is included. The project is being implemented on a partnership basis: in Eastern Cape, the Provincial Libraries and Information Service is the implementing channel, but Book Aid International (BAI) manages the project at the British end and an NGO, the Institute of Training and Education for Capacity-Building (ITEC), manages it in South Africa (Samuelson, 1997).

Determining factors

Contributors to the debate about the poor levels of reading materials and libraries in African schools (Ocholla, 1992; Ojiambo, 1988; Tawete, 1991) have tended to concentrate on problems such as the lack of properly trained personnel to develop effective library resources, absence of adequate and relevant stock, poor accommodation, and lack of official government policies and guidelines. But these problems are merely characteristics of the decay rather than its causes. They do not explain why governments were enthusiastic about libraries immediately after Independence and why there has been a more recent resurgence of interest in the 1990s.

Government priorities

An immediate cause of the widespread collapse of school libraries in the mid-1970s was certainly the pressure on national education budgets, caused by the rapid increase in enrolments in the years after Independence (Buchan, 1992 and 1995). In many countries pupil populations quadrupled in ten or fifteen years. In Kenya, for example, primary enrolment increased 50% in just one year (1974/75) and in Nigeria, primary enrolment quadrupled every year from 1976 to 1978. As a result, the salary percentage of national budgets rose dramatically (95% – 98% was not uncommon), leaving insufficient money in recurrent budgets to fund other school requirements. Supplementary reading materials and libraries were a first casualty. Coupled with this was the economic devastation caused in many countries by the oil price rises of the early 1970s. Foreign exchange reserves were reduced at a time when these were needed to fund book imports, paper and spare parts for printing machinery.

Confidence within Africa in education has been severely dented by the growing unemployment of school leavers. It seems that education is not providing the knowledge and skills that African countries require. In such circumstances, it is not surprising that little investment in the provision of reading materials has been made. However, attitudes to education are changing and governments are approaching education in a different way. The current emphasis is to move away from a centralized curriculum towards a learning process that is better matched to the needs of the individual and the community. There are efforts to make education more relevant, with a stress on 'know-how' and 'skills'. Of course, emphasis on the process of education is not new to Africa, but there is certainly a renaissance at the moment. South Africa is an example. The new national curriculum for the 21st century will effect a shift from a contents-based to an outcomes-based education. Education is seen as providing the conceptual tools necessary for creative and independent thought. It enshrines the principles of learner-centredness. Ministers of Education of 53 African countries met in Durban in April 1998 and confirmed their commitment to this new approach to education. In such systems, access to a wide-range of learning materials is a critical and essential component and not an optional luxury. It is therefore not surprising that many governments are now committing themselves (at least in theory) to policies supporting libraries in schools.

Publishing

Provision of supplementary reading materials in schools depends on a supply of relevant publications. Until the 1990s production of books for young people (apart from textbooks) was weak in most African countries and non-existent in others (Faye, 1998).

Since around 1987, there has been a spectacular growth in children's publishing, in both European and African languages. The number of titles published has exploded. One publisher in Kenya produced five titles in 1988 and 127 in 1998. Print runs now average between 3,000 and 5,000 per title. Standards are improving.

Books need to be sold and it is only the library market that can provide that necessary base on which local publishing can thrive and develop (Read, 1992). Publishers are now pressing for the development of libraries. The relationship between the two sectors is recognized as being symbiotic.

Funding agency attitudes and support

The pattern of supplementary materials provision in schools – its rise after Independence, its subsequent decline and the present renewed interest – has been most crucially determined by funding agency programmes.

The initial rapid educational development at Independence was heavily influenced by UNESCO ideals of universal primary education. There was also a demand for new books which would reflect national aspirations and the culture of newly independent nations. UNESCO supported library development; library support schemes were a standard part of the decolonization package offered by Britain to its former colonies. Its global Library Development Scheme operated until 1981. Libraries were seen as a way of strengthening democracy and consolidating favourable attitudes towards the mother country.

Towards the end of the 1970s, the World Bank identified textbooks as being the most cost-effective investment in upgrading educational achievement in poorer countries. Donors concentrated on financing textbook projects. A number of schemes were established concerned with textbook publishing, printing, distribution and policies. But the concentration on textbooks was done at the expense of supplementary reading materials. Such provision was ignored; no funding was made available and libraries decayed.

By the mid-1980s, the World Bank was moving towards a more comprehensive approach to book provision (Searle, 1985). It recognized that the provision of books needs to take everything into account, whether it be authorship capacity, publishing, distribution and access. Textbook provision alone could not revitalize education. The concept of the book sector study was developed. And since then, there has been renewed interest and investment in supplementary reading materials projects. Aid agencies have not only invested in the development of indigenous publishing but also in schemes supporting the access and delivery of reading materials to schools. Some of these projects are detailed earlier in this chapter.

For access provision to rely on the vagaries and fashions of international aid is a dangerous situation for African countries. It means that systems have not developed genuinely out of needs. Although books are procured and delivered to schools, this does not necessarily provide the basis for a reliable and sustainable system of book and information provision, once the aid ceases.

Chapter Three

SCHOOL LIBRARY SERVICES: GHANA AND TANZANIA
DIANA ROSENBERG

A school library service is a system which directs and assists the development of libraries in schools on a national or regional basis. At a minimum it involves the setting of policy and standards of provision plus advice on the establishment and maintenance of libraries. It can also offer assistance in the selection of stock, the acquisition, processing and distribution of books and journals and the training of staff. Such a service can be located within a public library or in a Ministry of Education; or sometimes it is the result of collaboration between the two.

Origins of school library services in Africa

In Sub-Saharan Africa (excluding South Africa), the concept of the school library service was introduced to Anglophone countries at the time of Independence and was linked to the establishment of public library systems. This followed the examples provided by the United Kingdom and South Africa. In the latter country, school libraries were (until the 1950s) seen as an integral part of the public library service. And the UK government recommended that there be a school library service arm to any national library service that was set up with its support at Independence. So the Jamaica Library Service in 1952 established a centralized schools service and the 1960 Hockey Report on the development of library services in East Africa recommended likewise. There was a general consensus that the reason for the poor state of school libraries in most of the developing world was the lack of central direction and no clearly defined policy on their development strategy. It was also recognized that the involvement of public libraries in the development of school libraries would be of mutual benefit, since it is the graduates of the school system who form the backbone of future public library services readership. Co-ordination and centralization were also seen as the most economic use of the scarce resources of trained staff and reading materials.

Ghana

In Ghana, although school libraries were never made the legal responsibility of the public library service, from its inception the Ghana Library Board (GLB) showed itself keen to assist the Ministry of Education. From 1959, the Library Board, at the request of the Ministry, operated a mobile library service to middle schools. But it became obvious that school libraries needed far more help than the occasional loan of additional books. With the exception of a few, all were in need of development grants, adequate accommodation and advice on selection and routines. A Working Committee, with members from the Library Board, the Ministry and the British Council, was set up in 1967 to carry out a survey of school libraries in secondary schools and teacher training colleges. It concluded that the main problem was the lack of any clearly defined policy, the haphazard nature of library provision and the poor staffing situation. As an interim measure, a librarian from the Voluntary Service Overseas (VSO – UK) was recruited as a School Library officer in Ashanti and workshops held for teacher-librarians. But the lack of any library consciousness in institutions of learning still prevailed. Any improvements were temporary and libraries tended to deteriorate after visits.

It became clear that something more long-term and far-reaching was required. In 1972, the Ghana Library Board decided to establish a Schools and Colleges Department (SCD) at its headquarters in Accra. This Department was given the responsibility to advise and assist in the establishment of good and effective libraries in secondary schools and teacher training colleges throughout Ghana. The overhead costs of running the service were met by the Library Board, with the Ministry of Education providing money for the purchase of books and journals for the school libraries.

Tanzania

Unlike the Ghana Library Board, Tanzania Library Services (TLS) was given the legal mandate to revitalize and develop special, school, college, government and public libraries into a single, integrated national library system. Therefore a school library service was on the agenda from 1961 and President Nyerere, when he opened the headquarters of the Tanzania Library Services in 1967, made a point of emphasizing that the development of school libraries was one of its key responsibilities.

Given the inadequate funds and insufficient trained personnel at its disposal, Tanzania Library Services had to decide what sort of school library service it could offer. It examined two possible options — to target all schools with a small amount of aid or to limit aid to a small number of schools, to which a reasonable service could be offered and which could become demonstration libraries. The latter method was adopted and, with the help of UNESCO, an expert in school library work was recruited in 1968. The establishment of the School Library Service (SLS), with its headquarters in the National Central Library in Dar es Salaam, was financed within the 2nd 5-year Development Plan, 1969–1974.

Activities and achievements

The ultimate aims of both the Ghana Library Board and Tanzania Library Services in their service to schools were very similar. Both restricted their work to the secondary level, although the former encompassed all schools, whilst the latter initially concentrated on establishing model schools. The aims were:

- to advise schools on the organization and running of their libraries, through means of regular visits and other professional assistance;
- to organize seminars, workshops and in-service training for school library personnel;
- to upgrade collections though the building up of standard collections, the loaning of material and the provision of reading lists;
- to order, process and distribute books and journals.

Ghana

The first ten years were ones of steady growth. The number of institutions participating in the programmes of the Schools and Colleges Department rose from 120 in 1972, to 245 in 1975, to 350 at the end of 1978. Activities included:

- **Visits** In the first year 226 library visits were made and advice offered on re-organization to meet professional standards.
- **Information** A book list of recommended titles and a manual on the organization and operation of libraries were published and distributed.
- **Training** Numerous training courses for teacher-librarians and in-service courses for school library assistants were mounted.
- **Model libraries** A model school library was opened at Accra High School in 1974, with the objective of improving stan-

dards in school libraries in Accra. A School Library Resource Centre at Aburi Girls Secondary School was set up in conjunction with the Department of Library and Archival Studies at the University of Ghana. One of the intentions was to monitor the effect of library services on student achievement.

- **Materials** Books and journals were purchased centrally, processed and distributed.

To run this service, the Ghana Library Board employed (as at 1981) a staff of four professionals, led by an Assistant Director, and 22 non-professionals. It was assisted financially by the British Council (which, for example, provided two years of periodical subscriptions and £5,000 to purchase books for the model library) and the Ghana Ministry of Education, which granted money for the purchase of books and journals (for example, US$100,000 in 1975 for books and £18,000 in 1978 for periodical subscriptions).

Since 1982, achievements have not been so spectacular. Although the number of institutions officially participating in the programme stood at 494 in 1991, the value of what is now provided is in some doubt. Alemna, writing in 1996, goes so far as to say that the Schools and Colleges Department exists almost in name only.

Activities have greatly reduced. Some of the duties proposed in 1972, such as advice to architects in the design of school libraries, the setting up of a central rebinding service, the formation of a School Library Association, were never really addressed from the start. But even advisory visits, training courses and the purchase and distribution of books and journals, frequent during the early years, are now few and far between. Between 1990 and 1997, only the following activities were undertaken:

- four advisory visits to schools;
- five training courses for school library staff;
- 13,000 books and 350 journals purchased and distributed;
- 39,400 donated books distributed.

Staff has also been drastically reduced, compared to the early years. In 1985, there was a total of eleven staff working in the Department, in 1995 there were thirteen, i.e. around half of the 1981 figure of 26. Underfunding is also a problem. The Library Board only provides the Schools and Colleges Department with a small advance to cover the operational costs of the Department. Any money for purchasing books and journals must come from those schools which choose to pay their library grants to the Library Board. In 1985, the equivalent of US$7,190 was received; in 1995 only US$480.

Events are overtaking the Schools and Colleges Department and its role. Partly as a recognition of the Department's poor performance, the Ministry of Education in 1986 set up a Community Libraries Project; one of its aims being to improve the standard of education of school pupils in the country (Alemna, 1996). In Accra alone there are nine community libraries. Such libraries act as supplements for the poor school libraries and inadequate home libraries. However, their success has been limited by poor finance, lack of materials and lack of trained staff. Another development is the establishment of the Ghana Book Trust, an NGO operating exclusively for charitable and educational purposes. It supplies books to schools and libraries throughout the country. It has also helped in the training of library assistants for these libraries. Enhancing access to information is no longer seen to be only the province of government.

Nevertheless, although the activities and influence of the Schools and Colleges Department would appear to be on the wane, its impact on the improvement of school libraries in Ghana must be given due recognition. A teacher-librarian interviewed during the data collection, considered that the training courses offered for school librarians and the processing and distribution of materials for school libraries had definitely helped to improve services. More such training courses were wanted, together with a closer supervision of what went on in the school libraries. Overall school libraries were better organized now, than before the establishment of the Schools and Colleges Department. Its very existence had helped to introduce the concept and purpose of the school library.

Tanzania

The UNESCO adviser had two tasks:
- to establish, in selected schools, model school libraries to serve as examples for teachers throughout the country;
- to provide assistance and advice to teachers in the selection of books and the operation of school libraries.

Each model library would be used to demonstrate:
- well-selected materials and their effects;
- the use that can be made of a library;
- the value of a library to the total development of the school pupil;
- purpose-built accommodation, furniture and equipment;
- good library organization.

In effect only three model libraries were established, one in each of three regions out of the twenty there were at the time.

The model library route was soon seen as being slow to produce results on the ground. Therefore, in 1971, a pilot school mobile library service was started, serving four regions: Mbeya, Iringa, Morogoro and Dodoma. This aimed to reinforce the book stock of all school libraries in an area, with visits two or three times a year for book return and selection.

At the same time efforts were made to improve the resources and organization of school libraries all over Tanzania:

- recommended book lists for secondary schools were produced and updates issued every three months;
- a list of recommended periodicals was published;
- a manual of library organization was published;
- minimum standards and a list of basic books in each subject were compiled;
- courses were run for teacher librarians;
- designs for school libraries and drawings of basic equipment were made available.

In addition, to try and overcome the staffing problem, a Certificate in Librarianship course was started by the Library Services in 1972. It was hoped that this would train school library assistants.

The School Library Service was mainly financed by Tanzania Library Services from government funds. In the Second Development Plan, 18% of the budget was allocated to the School Library Service. Help was also received from UNESCO, in particular for the first member of the staff. Up to 1976, the School Library Service was run by one professional and one library assistant.

Expansion of the School Library Service stopped in 1976. In the Third 5-year Development Plan, 1976–1981, nothing was planned and nothing took place. No more model libraries were opened (the plan had been to start one in each of the 20 regions of Tanzania) and no more regions were served by the mobile service. The planned centralization of acquisition, processing and distribution of books was never started. Primary schools were never included (although they could apply for book boxes from the Extension Branch of Tanzania Library Services).

Even the operations of the existing service were barely maintained. Although staffing levels were retained and even increased (in 1995 it was staffed by one professional librarian, three paraprofessional library assistants and one library attendant), funding was reduced to a bare minimum. Records are not available, as the Library Services do not publish expenditure for individual departments or divisions. But, in an interview during the data collection, the former Deputy Director General of the Library Services admitted that the the School Library Service programmes were severely affected by the inadequate government subventions from the early '80s onwards. And in the 1992/93 financial year, no expenses for the School Library Service other than salaries were covered by the Tanzania Library Services budget.

Nevertheless, the School Library Service still exists. Between 1990 and 1997 it:

- made six advisory visits;
- published eight lists of recommended books;
- purchased and distributed 2,250 books and journals;
- distributed 112,000 donated books and journals;
- reissued the manual on library procedures.

The School Mobile Library had long since been grounded. And although general training for library assistants was offered (the National Library Assistants' Certificate Course, in-service training, etc.), none was directed at the specific needs of teacher-librarians or school administrators. The main function of the School Library Service today would seem to be that of an agency for receiving and distributing donated materials.

By 1985, the Tanzania Library Service was admitting that its much vaunted supportive services to schools had been curtailed. In that year, the Deputy Director wrote: 'Tanzania Library Service is a large organization. Its operations are national and it has many commitments. The services it provides to schools are therefore very minimal' (Ilomo, 1985). The School Library Service was no longer seen as one of the top priorities of the Library Services. In the same paper, Ilomo suggests three approaches to work with schools:

- developing and maintaining professional standards and awareness, in co-operation with the Ministry of National Education;
- on the spot guidance and assistance in the establishment, organization and management of school libraries, on request;
- provision of a School Mobile Library to four regions.

More recently, the government of Tanzania has introduced new strategies to revive school libraries. The Sectoral Development Policy for Education, which has library components, is one of those recent efforts. The government has realized that operationally the Library Services cannot manage all school library activities. In its plan to establish school libraries in all schools in Tanzania, the role of a the School Library Service will be held by the Ministry of Education and Culture, in conjunction with local authorities. The role of the Tanzania Library Services will be limited to advisory services, development and maintenance of standards and manuals and maintenance of professionalism (information from interviews in 1997 with the former Deputy Director General and with the Chief Librarian of the Tanzania Library Services).

At the same time, those interviewed in 1997 generally agreed that the School Library Service had resulted in some improvements. The consultation services provided by the Tanzania Library Services had benefited a number of schools, particularly in the private sector. And the fact the Ministry of Education and Culture had recently introduced a new strategy to revive school libraries, suggests that it has realized that they are important to the educational process.

Reasons for failure

Despite initial enthusiasm for the concept, school library services in Africa have failed to maintain their early promise. The activities of those that were established declined; this is true not only for Ghana and Tanzania but also for Nigeria, where three State Public Library Boards had set up School Library Services in the 1970s. In other countries, like Kenya and Uganda, a school library service never left the drawing board. Lack of money is usually given for their ultimate failure. And Ilomo, writing in 1985, concluded that financial limitation was the main obstacle. Finance certainly played a part, but this reason is often used to disguise the existence of other crucial factors. Furthermore, the availability of finance does not necessarily mean that it will be channeled to the development of school libraries. Nigeria in the 1980s was rich with oil money; libraries in universities benefited, but those in schools continued to decline (Alemna, 1990).

Ghana

School libraries in Ghana still 'face a myriad of problems' and these are not being solved by the Schools and Colleges Department (Alemna, 1990). A regional librarian, interviewed during the collection of data in Ghana, said that the main way of improving the performance of the Schools and Colleges Department would be to provide an increase in funding and, as a result, in materials for schools. However, those writers who have analyzed the situation place far more weight on the failure over the years to convince educational planners and administrators and the teaching profession as a whole that school libraries are a necessity and not a luxury. The same regional librarian also admitted that school libraries are deteriorating because of lack of government attention and low interest from administrators. Reasons given for the overall lack of impact of the Schools and Colleges Department are:

- Official interest in libraries has been 'cool and casual, rather than active and sustained' (Alemna, 1996). This lack of commitment by government and lack of interest by school principals and heads is seen as the main reason why standards (neither those laid down in the 1972 Manual for School Libraries in Ghana, nor those proposed by Alemna in 1993) have not been adopted, legislation has not been introduced, and monies allocated to libraries have often been diverted for other purposes. There is no specific training requirement for school librarians in Ghana. The resulting use of unqualified staff has led to poor services and libraries which do not add to the quality of education offered in the schools. Evidence to convince those in power positions on the importance of libraries has not been made available. Alemna, writing in 1994, commented that no-one appeared to be in a position to give any clear indication as to whether the growth of organized library services in schools had any impact on the poor reading habits of school leavers – which was the key reason for setting up the Schools and Colleges Department in the first place. Even the introduction of a new educational system in Ghana in 1986, one that demanded greater use of books and libraries, did not result in more support for the Schools and Colleges Department and its role in developing school libraries.
- The Schools and Colleges Department has always been in an ambiguous position organizationally. Its operational status, *vis à vis* both the Ghana Library Board and the Ministry of Education, has never been clearly defined for the purposes of co-ordination. Without a secure source of funding, it has been difficult to plan long-term programmes. The Department has always led a hand-to-mouth existence. What is needed is a School Libraries Division within the Ministry of Education, with which the Schools and Colleges Department could co-operate.
- Any school library needs an adequate and ongoing supply of relevant books and journals. Appropriate material needs to be produced locally and until there is a viable local publishing industry producing such material and in suffi-cient quantities, it will always be difficult to stock school libraries. Reliance on imported and donated material from outside the country is not a viable option.

Given the very evident failure of the Schools and Colleges Department to continue to develop and support school libraries in Ghana, it was dispiriting to find that there are no current plans to alter or change its role to make it more functionally relevant to the problems faced by school libraries.

Tanzania

Asked about the current state of school libraries in Tanzania, interviewees said that the libraries in government-owned primary and secondary schools were dead. The few existing school libraries in Tanzania were run by private organizations. The situation in 1997 was much the same as it had been thirty years earlier, when the School Library Service was just starting. The latter had had little impact.

Misgivings about the likely impact of Tanzania's School Library Service were voiced early on in its life, both by Miss Taylor, the last expatriate head of the School Library Service, and the Director of the Tanzania Library Services, Mr Kaungamno. The overriding problem was that schools themselves had to want and to recognize the need for libraries, to consider that a well-stocked and well-organized library was essential for teaching and learning. Only then would a part of the *per capita* grant given to each school be reserved for library expenditure. Only then would schools see the need to appoint permanent trained library staff, to ensure control and continuity, rather than rely on teachers, who were frequently transferred and, anyway, had other duties to perform. As it was, the education curriculum was biased towards formal instruction and teachers expected only textbooks to be read; broad reading was not encouraged. Unless there was a change of attitude towards libraries, no lessons could be learnt from model libraries. Mobile libraries could only supplement a school's own collection; the latter had to be at least adequate. Advice and training was of little use if it fell on deaf ears. In short, it was not possible to impose libraries on schools.

These same reasons were reiterated by those interviewed in 1997. Although the Tanzania Library Services had the legal mandate to develop school libraries, it was recognized that the momentum must come from the Ministry of Education and, in the schools, from the headteachers. It was essential that the coordinator of any the School Library Service should be based in the Ministry. Only teachers and school administrators could provide the opportunities for librarians to speak on the importance of school libraries and how they might be used to enhance the education process.

Of course funding or lack of it was also given as a reason for the failure of the School Library Service to maintain its services, whether in the purchase of books, the running of the mobile service or even at the very basic level of making transport available for librarians to visit schools.

Another reason was that, as in Ghana, the local book industry needed to be developed, so as to provide materials which were relevant and appropriate to the school population at a reasonable price.

Evaluation and conclusions

Despite its relative lack of success in practice, the school library concept remains a popular solution for ensuring access to reading materials. The Director of the Tanzania Library Services (as late as 1979) declared that the experience of Africa had proved that a school library service is the right course of action, with the national library service taking the lead. And for countries like Kenya, which never managed to establish such a service, the call throughout the 1980s was for a definite government policy, enshrining standards in terms of library buildings, books, equipment and staff and for these to be implemented through the development of a comprehensive school library service. But the continuing deplorable state of school libraries is leading to a more realistic approach. It is recognized that Tanzania, where the legal responsibilities are clearly spelled out, has not managed to overcome problems. Whereas a Workshop on School Libraries at the 1984 IFLA Conference still favoured the development of school library services, an IFLA Seminar in 1993 was more cautious. Yes, an explicit government policy and training for those running school libraries was considered necessary. But co-operation and collaboration with other libraries rather than the setting up of a school library service was recommended. And the encouragement of a local publishing industry, so that relevant reading materials were easily available, was thought to be equally important.

Certainly the experiences of school library services in Ghana and Tanzania tend to support these conclusions. One thing that comes out very clearly is that any such service, whether comprehensive or limited in its objectives, must be based in the Ministry of Education rather than a national library service or public library. It must have the total commitment of that Ministry; it must arise from the expressed needs of school heads and administrators; it must be recognized as an essential part of the education process; its programmes must dovetail with the teaching programmes. Only then will it stand a chance of receiving financial support. Once established, such a service can then request co-operation from other libraries, for example in establishing standards or in training of staff to run the libraries.

Another conclusion is that a school library service, however comprehensive, can only supplement the library that is established and maintained by the school. The need for libraries has to be accepted by both teachers and parents; their value (e.g. in improving examination results) has to be demonstrable. The support offered by a school library service has to be demand-led. Libraries are bottom-up rather than top-down operations; they are the result of community need. Only then will financial support (through, for example, parental contributions on pupil enrolment or charity walks organized by the school – suggestions made by interviewees in Tanzania) be forthcoming.

A school library service presupposes that school libraries in each school are the best way of providing access to reading materials. Of the two countries studied, Ghana is now moving towards community libraries as an alternative. And Tanzania has experimented with joint school-public libraries. Maybe the answer may lie in co-operation between different types of libraries and taking advantage of what exists.

One advantage of a school library service is that it should benefit from economies of scale: centralized training, rotating book collections, expert advice. However, in practice in Africa, such a service seems to have become an expensive and not very effective additional layer of bureaucracy. And when funds for the purchase of reading materials are in such short supply, it is hard to defend the existence of this extra layer. To pay the salaries of thirteen staff (as in Ghana) to make four advisory visits to schools, run five training courses and distribute a small number of books over a period of the last seven years is not cost effective. And the same is true for Tanzania, where five staff only managed to make six visits, publish eight reading lists and again purchase and distribute a relatively small number of books over the seven years. Among those interviewed, the centralized services that were most valued by the schools were expert advice and the provision of specialized training courses for school librarians. Perhaps these could be provided more cost effectively by small non-governmental bodies set up for that specific purpose, such as the Ghana Book Trust and, in Senegal, Bibliothèque–Lecture–Développement (BLD).

A final conclusion is that school libraries are there to provide supplementary reading materials. Some of this material may come from outside the country and through donations; at the moment most of the material distributed in Ghana and Tanzania is composed of donations from abroad. But the core, if it is to be relevant to school age needs, must be published and available locally. This requires a vibrant local book industry. If this is lacking, then the contribution of any school library to education will be drastically reduced.

Chapter Four

SCHOOL LIBRARIES: MALI
AMADOU BÉKAYE SIDIBÉ

Background

Socio-economic and political context

Mali is a landlocked country situated in the heart of West Africa. According to the 1994 census it had a population of 10,443,000, 25.5% of whom were under 15 years of age. The bulk of this population is rural (74% as against 26% urban population). It is made up of such ethnic groups as the Bambara, Fula, Senufo, Bobo, Tuareg, etc. which give the country an unparalleled diversity and cultural richness.

Economically, Mali is a very poor country. In 1994 the Gross National Product (GNP) was estimated at US$1,871 million and the *per capita* income at US$250. Since 1982 Mali has been subject to an International Monetary Fund structural adjustment programme. This programme has obliged and encouraged many state employees to take retirement. It has also led to the introduction of an entry competition to slow down the influx of young graduates into the civil service. Consequently librarianship is suffering from a shortage of specialists: instead of recruiting new staff, the authorities prefer to make transfers within the administrative or teaching staff to provide management for the libraries.

From a historical viewpoint, Mali is the heir to great empires, such as that of Ghana in the 13th century. In the 10th and 11th centuries, Islam began to enter the northern part of the country, becoming strongly established there. In the 14th and 15th centuries relations with the Arab world were enriched and consolidated. It was at this time that Mali established its first universities, for example the University of Timbuktu. Those centuries also saw its first great writers and translators of Arabic documents.

In 1850 the systematic colonization of Africa began. French colonizers gradually invaded Malian territory and despoiled the country of most of its cultural wealth. Precious copies of the

Koran, for example, were carried off. Between 1909 and 1915 revolts broke out but these were unable to overthrow the colonial government. On 17 January 1959, Mali and Senegal formed a federation, which declared Independence in June 1960. In August the federation broke down and Mali gained Independence on 22 September 1960.

In 1962 the first president, Modibo Keita, reformed the educational system, a reform which became the cornerstone of education in Mali. In 1968 Modibo Keita was overthrown by the military, headed by Moussa Traoré. On 26 March 1991 the people once again revolted and overthrew the regime of Moussa Traoré. Multi-partyism was introduced and the press diversified. People once again began to hope to see all the country's children getting an education.

Educational policies and practices

Mali inherited an inadequate educational system which was designed to train administrators and clerks within the colonial system. The ambition was not to promote and extend education to the indigenous population but to train assistants.

On gaining Independence, Mali needed to train managers to ensure its administration and run its economy, in short, to make its Independence effective – that required effective, rapid, mass education. The education reforms of 1962 set out five general principles:

1 Quality mass education
2 An education system that could provide a management tier within the financial and time constraints allowed by the country's development plans
3 Education to guarantee a cultural level that would enable Malian qualifications to be as good as those of modern states
4 Education whose content was based not only on specifically African and Malian values but also on universal values
5 Education that decolonized minds

The 1962 reforms were further revised and corrected in 1964 by the first seminar on education which recommended:
• adapting curricula to national realities;
• directing pupils towards the rural sector from the end of primary education;
• strengthening technical training.

The basic level of education in Mali is made up of two cycles:
1 the first cycle lasting six years which ends with an examination and the issuing of the Certificate of Primary Studies (CEP);

2 the second cycle of three years which also ends with an examination and the issuing of a Diploma of Basic Studies.

The task of reforming the schools and education system was not easy since the post-colonial education heritage was very meagre. In 1959, for example, Mali had 351 schools with 1,183 classes: 54,136 pupils were studying in the first cycle out of a school-age population of 569,700. There were 1,080 pupils in the second cycle, and 111 students at higher level in France and in Dakar. The percentage of enrolment amongst the school-age population was 9.5%, the lowest in French West Africa.

However, with the help of the Soviet Union the reform soon bore fruit, as shown in Table 4.1.

Table 4.1 School enrolment at basic level, 1959–1968 (end of rule of Modibo Keita)

Year	No. of classes	No. of pupils in 1st cycle	No. of pupils in 2nd cycle	% of school population enrolled
1959	1 183	54 136	1 080	9.5%
1962	1 504	67 643	4 987	n/a
1964	2 233	102 851	17 044	19%
1968	4 298	156 967	29 055	22.4%

The percentage enrolled in schools rose from 9.5% to 22.4% in nine years, a remarkable achievement. And yet this success was short-lived. Galloping population growth and economic difficulties created a gap between the people and the ruling US-RDA party. The schools suffered the effects of this.

In 1968 the military took power and the quest for lasting solutions to the education crisis began. With this aim in mind, Malian schools underwent numerous reforms (in 1970, 1978, 1985). Between 1968 and 1991 the school enrolment ratio varied between 18.9% and 27.56%. In 1978 the government allocated 14% of the national budget to education. But despite these efforts the schools continued to decline. Student strikes became more common. Teachers in some areas went months without being paid. Many teachers migrated to neighbouring countries such as Côte d'Ivoire and Gabon to find paid work. Currently the Tokten programme (United Nations Development Programme) is funding the involvement of this diaspora in building the country.

In 1995 there were 1,523 public and 209 private schools for the first cycle and 264 public and 17 private schools for the second cycle. In the same year, the first cycle had 8,162 teachers and there were 552,891 pupils, an average of 52 to 69 pupils per class in the different year groups.

Education at the secondary level lasts three years in the lycées and two to four years in the professional schools. The lycées prepare pupils for university entrance while the professional schools offer training in such subjects as accountancy, building, business studies, etc.

Since 1991 there have been many seminars on education; recommendations have been made and they are in the process of being implemented. For example, in 1996 an action plan was adopted to reduce the repetition rate from 30% to 15%, and to reach a pupil enrolment rate of 50%. Table 4.2 shows exam pass rates.

Table 4.2 Pass rates at end of cycle examinations

	1st cycle	2nd cycle
1987	12%	12%
1988	49%	35%
1994	58%	41%
1995	59%	48%

Major efforts are currently being made to increase the number of schools. At the secondary level, five lycées were opened between 1995 and 1997, bringing the total to 19. However, it is generally agreed that although pass rates are improving, the overall quality of education is deteriorating. The repetition rate remains high (28%), as does the rate of exclusion. Today, amongst the many problems that Malian schools are facing, the most serious one remains strikes. Since 1991 these strikes have meant that schools have not been able to get through the curriculum. There is no point drawing up valuable curricula if they cannot be fully implemented.

Information provision

Libraries in Mali have tended to be privileged places of cultural development and to be concentrated in Bamako, the capital. School pupils there have access to the libraries provided by the French and American Cultural Centres, specialist children's libraries and the National Library. In 1997, OLP (Opération Lecture Publique – Popular Reading Programme) was launched. It is a Franco–Malian project, supported financially by the French Co-operation Mission, located in the Division of Cultural Heritage within the National Directorate of Arts and Culture. Its aim is to promote reading throughout Mali by setting up a public library in each of the 46 administrative divisions into which Mali was then divided and to train librarians to manage the libraries.

44   Small reading and activity centres for children have been set up by Opération Lecture Publique in some localities, but their functioning is not very effective. More successful in meeting the needs of children has been a project establishing centres for promoting children's reading (CLAEC – Centres de Lecture et d'Animation pour les Enfants) which are the result of a twinning agreement between Bamako and Angers in France. Angers has created and equipped six CLAECs in the six communes of Bamako. The communes, on their part, agree to upkeep the premises, provide staff and maintain the services. There is a management section in each commune. The libraries are well used by school children from the first cycle. There are also children's libraries within the National Library (initiated by Operation Lecture Publique) and the French Cultural Centre.

The National Library is open to all. Home loan is possible on registration. An examination of loan records over a fortnight during this survey showed that 35 loans had been made by school pupils, mainly from nearby lycées and predominantly by those studying the sciences.

School libraries

The earliest schools in Mali (which was then known as French Sudan) came into existence at the end of the 19th century. With the advent of Independence in 1960 and especially after the 1962 reform, these schools were reformed and adapted to the new demands. For example, the Collège Technique became the Lycée Technique, the Ecole d'Administration du Soudan became the Ecole Nationale d'Administration. New schools were built. But it was not until the 1970s that the first school libraries appeared. Today, a look at what has happened to these libraries leads us to a bitter conclusion. For schools at the basic level, libraries are virtually non-existent. The few information units that do exist in them lack suitable premises. Nor are they managed by professional librarians. The libraries of the first and second cycles of basic education are often made up of 50 to 100 items kept in a cupboard or two in the head's office. Use of them amounts to no more than the distribution of such items as are available amongst pupils at the beginning of the school year. The number of items is totally insufficient, and so one textbook is given to two or even three pupils whose families live near one another. The pupils, usually those in examination classes, who thus enjoy an annual home loan, must return the items borrowed before the last tests. The holdings of libraries are enriched by gifts from twinned towns or schools. There is minimal participation by the Ministry of Basic Education in the constitution of these information units.

At the secondary level, the situation is less dramatic. Most institutions at this level have a library. There are however a few exceptions which do not. Amongst these are the Lycée D. Konaré in Kayes, whose library was burned down by the pupils in 1996, the five new lycées and some private lycées (Lycée Konary, for example). But the schools which have libraries suffer from the same problems as their counterparts at the basic level, that is:

- lack of suitable premises;
- total lack of a budget;
- lack of a professional librarian;
- lack of chances for in-service training opportunities for librarians;
- lack of co-operation between them and international bodies or bodies in other countries.

Relations with the outside world are limited to those maintained with twinned towns or schools. Most of the librarians in the basic and secondary cycles are unaware of the International Federation of Library Associations (IFLA) and therefore have never enjoyed the services of that body. Although the libraries of the secondary level are members of AMBAD (Association Malienne des Bibliothécaires, Archivistes et Documentalistes — Malian Association of Librarians, Archivists and Documentalists), this association has been able to achieve little for lack of funds.

Methodology

For this survey the library collections of Ecole Nationale d'Administration, Centre Djoliba, and the National Office for Statistics and Information were searched for general information on Mali and on its education system. Interviews were made with the Directors of Studies, librarians and pupils of those lycées which had been selected for case studies. Information was also obtained from pupils with the help of a questionnaire, see the Appendix.

In fact, until now, nothing has been written about school libraries in Mali. It is hoped that this research will provide a basis for further research.

'A library in every school' programme

This new programme aims to establish libraries in schools at the basic level, where, as we have seen, there is little or no access to reading materials.

Origins

Until the 1990s there was no planned creation of libraries at the basic level. It is only in the last few years that Opération Lecture Publique (OLP), which had already achieved its main targets in the public library field, began creating some libraries in schools, with the support of the local population. In this way twenty libraries were built and equipped all over the country, such as the library in the school at Missira in Bamako.

But OLP, which does not come under the Ministry of National Education, had insufficient funds to carry on creating libraries in schools since it depended on the French Co-operation Mission. It felt it was necessary to combine its efforts with those of the Ministry of Education where the idea of 'A library in every school' had already taken root. In doing so, the original concept of the Ministry of Education was considerably improved. Whilst initially it consisted of equipping each school with a book cupboard, it now means the creation of a library in the full sense of the word.

Opération Lecture Publique sought funding from the French Co-operation Mission for the new project. The Mission approved the request and a protocol of agreement was signed between it, the Ministry of Basic Education, the OLP and the Comité Editorial Bamakois (CEBA) on 15 March 1997. The OLP provides the technical aspect of the programme. A unit responsible for the Management of Libraries in Basic Schools was set up. Initially, given the shortage of funds, the management unit set the short-term target of creating ten school libraries. Criteria were laid down for designating the schools that would be the first to benefit from these libraries. This programme is the first government structure for libraries at the basic level of education.

Criteria

In order to benefit from the creation of a library within the school, the latter must meet the following conditions:
- it must have first and second cycles;
- the local community must provide:
  - appropriate premises to house the library
  - twenty chairs and two reading tables
  - two sets of shelves;
- the school must nominate a librarian from among the teachers.

Through the management unit, the programme looks after the training in documentary techniques of the teacher who is nominated. It also endows the library with 255 books and ensures the co-ordination of all the libraries in the network.

Despite these constraining conditions for schools and their localities, demand for libraries has been very strong. The communities have shown themselves happy to commit themselves to the programme and they have done so to the satisfaction of the programme decision-makers. An example of this commitment is Torokorobougou, a district of Bamako, which equipped a splendid room for its school library, costing over US$2,000.

Finance

On the one hand, the programme is funded by the French Co-operation Mission. This institution funds the OLP and the whole network of libraries that this embraces. The Réseau Malien de Documentation (REMADOC) is also dependent on it. For 'A library in every school' programme, the Mission made available to the unit a sum of 15 million CFA Francs (US$7,500.00). Of this sum 53.5% (8 million CFA Francs) will be devoted to the purchase of books. The rest will be invested in training librarians and in creating, equipping and operating the unit.

On the other hand, the programme is supported financially by the local community. This support from local people is vital if the programme's objectives are to be attained rapidly. This support need not be limited to satisfying the conditions laid down for schools to benefit from the creation of a library (chairs, tables, book shelves, etc.). The communities can go further if they have the means, for example by buying books on the spot. For that they could draw not only on their own resources but also on those of people from the areas who live in the big cities or overseas.

Current state of libraries in the programme

In less than a year after the launch of the programme, the people involved have made considerable efforts in providing facilities. According to Mr Tamboura, who is in charge of the unit, the ten libraries are already equipped, the librarians have all been through the training course and the first supply of 2,550 books will soon be delivered to the libraries. Of the books ordered, 18% (470 books) were provided by Malian publishers (Figuier, Jamana, DNAFLA, etc.). This not only supports the country's publishing industry but at the same time reduces the proportion of books not adapted to the Malian cultural context. The first, at Torokorobougou, was opened on 3 February 1998.

The distribution of the first libraries is uneven. As shown in Table 4.3, of the eight regions of Mali, only schools in five regions will receive a library in this first phase of the programme. The regions of Gao, Tombouctou (Timbuktu) and Kidal do not appear.

It is hoped that the second phase which envisages the creation of 20 new libraries will fill this gap.

Table 4.3 Distribution of first libraries in the 'A library in every school' project

District/Region	Locality/Quarter	Name of beneficiary school
Bamako	Torokorobougou	Ecole fondamentale de Torokorobougou
Kayes	Diamou	Ecole fondamentale de Diamou
	Seguela	Ecole fondamentale de Seguela
Koulikoro	Yelekebougou	Ecole fondamentale de Yelekebougou
Sikasso	Niéna	Ecole fondamentale de Niéna
	Kléla	Ecole fondamentale de Kléla
Ségou	Séribala	Ecole fondamentale de Séribala
Mopti	Dia	Ecole fondamentale de Dia
	Hombori	Ecole fondamentale de Hombori
	Sévaré	Ecole fondamentale de Sévaré

Evaluation

The libraries were not yet operational at the time of this survey and it is therefore not possible to provide data on user satisfaction, impact or long term sustainability. What however is apparent is that the local population, the teachers and the pupils much appreciate and encourage the establishment of libraries in the schools. All are aware of the importance of libraries and reading in the educational system. That is why, when talking about the low intellectual level of pupils, the parents all say that they do not read. This absence of a reading culture, especially at the basic level, is due not to a lack of will on the part of pupils but to the non-existence of access to reading materials. In a country such as Mali, where parents' income is quite inadequate to build up personal libraries for their children, the establishment of school libraries is bound to be supported.

On the other hand 'A library in every school' project is very ambitious given the state's limited means. Ten schools now have libraries; another 20 are planned. But there are over 1,700 schools at the first cycle and around 280 at the second cycle. And the creation of libraries in itself is meaningless if every effort is not made to supply them regularly with up-to-date items and materials and to ensure the continued training of their librarians. It is for that reason that the unit is currently seeking sponsors (NGOs, national or international associations, foundations, etc.) and donors. It hopes to establish fruitful and diversified long-term co-operation with them. Self-sustainability is not envisaged.

Libraries at the secondary level

Libraries in three secondary schools were examined for this survey: the Library of Lycée Askia Mohammed, the Library of the Lycée des Jeunes Filles and the Library of the Lycée Technique.

Library of Lycée Askia Mohammed

Lycée Askia Mohammed (LAM) is one of the leading educational institutions in Mali. It was established in 1915, long before Independence. Situated in Bamako, it is certainly the country's largest lycée. In 1997/98, Lycée Askia Mohammed had 2,170 pupils taught by 87 teachers. It has not been possible to establish the exact date of the establishment of the library at LAM, according to some sources it was set up in the 1970s. The LAM library is, of course, intended to meet the information needs of the pupils, teachers and administrative staff of the body which runs it.

COLLECTION DEVELOPMENT

The collection is very poor. It totals only 991 items, equal to 0.45 items per pupil. Subject distribution is given in Table 4.4. All areas are covered. The library does not subscribe to any jounals or periodicals.

The book stock increases essentially through gifts which are by definition irregular. It is therefore impossible to say by how much it is rising each year. According to one of the librarians, the library used to receive 300 items a year from the Bibliothèques Scolaires et Universitaires project (BSU – a book donation programme operating in Mali) initiated in 1984 by Operation Lecture Publique and the Department of National Education. This project ended in the mid-90s and since then the library has not received any items. In fact, over two-thirds of the stock is made up of items from the 1970s and 1980s.

STAFFING

There are two full-time librarians. They were trained on OLP's 15 day introduction to library management but they have not been on any training course since 1994.

PHYSICAL FACILITIES

The reading room is very small. It is poorly equipped and has only
51 chairs, nine reading tables and three cupboards. That means it

cannot even accommodate one-twentieth of the pupils. The books are arranged on five metal shelves. There is no manual card index for users. A loan desk is situated at the entrance to the library. The library has no typewriter which, had it existed, would have been of great help in preparing bibliographical slips and drafting correspondence.

Table 4.4 LAM library collection by subject

Subject	Number of items
General	143
Philosophy	80
Social sciences	118
Religion	3
Botany	7
Languages, linguistics	40
Exact sciences	170
Applied sciences	87
Zoology	9
Arts – fine arts, decorative arts	16
Music	12
Literature (including novels)	62
Leisure activities	24
History and geography	220
Total	**991**

SERVICES

There is direct access to the collection. All that the pupils have to do is present their valid student card in order to use the library's services. Users from outside the institution who are not pupils are required to present a valid civil card. The library is open when students are in class.

Despite the poverty of the library, use of the collection is regular and encouraging. The two librarians receive an average of 60 visitors a day. They give 37–43 consultations a day on the spot. There is not much home lending given the lack of stock and the desire to enable the maximum number of readers to benefit from the library's services. Lending is chiefly to teachers for the preparation of their courses.

The library does not produce any bibliography or leaflet to give readers information about its collection. The library is not computerized. There is no photocopier or binding equipment. That means that the library has no source of income.

USER SATISFACTION

A user survey was conducted on 30 pupils and 10 teachers. Readers were not satisfied with their library. Findings included:

- 98% felt that the collection was very poor. They also asserted that the little that does exist is too old and out-dated to meet current needs.
- 5% of those questioned said that the inability of the librarians to answer their questions satisfactorily has made them not come to the library. But, to be fair, the poor response to users' questions is not dependent solely on the intellectual ability of the librarian but also and above all on the quality of the collection, the level of co-operation between libraries and the means of communication available. To give a good reply it is of course necessary to know all about the collection and how to exploit sources of information (catalogues, manual card indexes, etc.) but information on what does not exist or which exists in other libraries can only be given if the means of doing so (catalogue, database of a network of libraries, etc.) are available.
- 61% stated that they were put off by the library's opening hours and by their irregularity. It has to be admitted that many librarians at the secondary level do not respect the opening times that they themselves set. Systematic lateness and early closing of libraries constitute a serious handicap for good user relations. Factors such as the lack of interest in the library on the part of the school authorities promote this behaviour on the part of librarians.
- None of the users questioned had received any training whatsoever on how to use libraries. (It should be pointed out that bibliography is only taught in the Faculty of Legal and Economic Sciences and the Faculty of Medicine.)
- The teachers approached all thought that the collection was very poor. The available items are read and re-read each year in order to give classes. That means that it is impossible for even the teachers to keep their knowledge up to date, let alone the pupils who are completely dependent on their notebooks. Because of the lack of documents, lectures cannot be given regularly.

To sum up, the findings of the survey showed that the most serious problems of the LAM library remain the poverty of the collection, the lack of opportunities for training and further training for librarians and the lack of co-operation with other libraries at the secondary level.

Library of the Lycée des Jeunes Filles (Lycée Ba Aminata Diallo)

The Lycée des Jeunes Filles (Girls' Lycée) in Bamako was established on 4 February 1951. In 1997/98 there were 1,789 pupils, taught by 88 teachers.

COLLECTION DEVELOPMENT

According to the stock register there are estimated to be 2,851 items. However, this figure needs to be revised downwards as the stock register does not reflect losses and withdrawals of items. Of this total number of items, 2,451 books have been recorded, processed and arranged in cupboards. The rest (400 books), after being recorded, were directly put on the shelves. The latter are made up solely of textbooks and are lent to students for home use during the school year. The collection covers such subjects as history, geography, mathematics, physics, chemistry, biology, languages (French, English, German, Russian), linguistics and philosophy.

The library has no budget of its own. It can therefore make no purchases of items even annually. The collection increases thanks to gifts. The chief donors are:

- **OLP** In the framework of the BSU book donation project, OLP used to give libraries 300 items a year. That project came ended in 1994 and since then the library of the Lycée des Jeunes Filles has had no source for acquiring items;
- **The Fondation Partage** In 1997 it made a gift of over 100 items to the library. These items deal with general culture. This same gesture was made to other school libraries and to a number of university libraries.

STAFFING

The library is managed on a day-to-day basis by three librarians, all teachers by training. These librarians attended a fortnight-long course given by OLP in 1985 and 1986. Since then none of them has attended any course whatsoever.

PHYSICAL FACILITIES

The library consists of a single room, which was renovated in 1986 by OLP. It is equipped with six reading tables, 36 chairs, six shelves, two cupboards and two work posts. A loan book keeps a check of home loans.

There is direct access to the collection and so there is no manual card index for users. Materials (pens, sticking tape, glue, covering, cards, labels, etc.) are supplied by OLP and the school management.

SERVICES

The library receives 30–40 visitors a day. It used to lend books on home loan for the whole school year. Such loans were recorded in the textbook register in which the name of the borrower was entered. Home loans have been halted because of the endless transfers of students and teachers to other establishments.

All readers may consult items on the spot. The busiest times continue to be the break and recreation times. However, the library is only open during school hours: 8.00 a.m. – midday and 3.00 – 5.00 p.m.

USER SATISFACTION

Group interviews and a survey were conducted to assess satisfaction with the stock and services of the library, which indicate that the collection is well used. Some textbooks are consulted two to four times a day. According to the loan register the use to which the collection is put is very high (80%).

Despite that, the percentage of dissatisfied users remained high:

- 90% considered the collection lacked the books they required. Because of this, the pupils cannot meet all the demands of academic life. For example, the lecture topics in lycées in literature are: the meeting of cultures, colonization, money, etc. It appears that none of these topics is sufficiently covered by the collection. This means that the teacher is forced to give the students more time so that everyone can read the one or two items recommended for the lecture. This state of affairs does not allow teachers to do the maximum of practical work so as to underpin the students' theoretical knowledge.
- 25% criticized the opening hours. They do not suit the readers. The fact that the library's opening hours are identical with those of classes makes it impossible for pupils to consult items on the spot. Home loans are not allowed and, even if they were, they would not have enabled all users to have access to the items that they want, because of the insufficient quantity of stock.
- 5% questioned the reception and competence of the librarians. This is a consequence not only of the inadequacy of the level of training but also of the poverty of the collection, the available sources of information and the lack of co-operation amongst libraries at the secondary level.

Library of the Lycée Technique

The Lycée Technique was founded in 1962 following the reform of the Collège Technique, which had been established in 1948 by the colonial government. The Lycée Technique is currently an institution with a good reputation. In 1997/98 it had 1,315 pupils. Courses are given by 94 teachers.

COLLECTION DEVELOPMENT

The library is estimated to contain 6,232 items covering a wide range of subjects including history and geography, reading, technology, mathematics, physics and chemistry. The collection is made up essentially of books (98%), but there are a few journals: *Le Courier, Cacao, Deutschland, Les Temps Nouveaux*, etc. The library does not subscribe to them, and they are not acquired on a regular basis. In addition to journals and books there are also 'bandes dessinées' (similar to comic strip books).

The collection is predominantly in French. However, there are a few items in English and German.

The collection is increasing thanks to gifts from OLP (the BSU project), the city of Angers (France), CODE (Canadian Organization for Development through Education) and individuals.

STAFFING

There is one librarian, who reports to the Director of Studies.

PHYSICAL FACILITIES

The library is not computerized. The room has 72 seats and fourteen reading tables. The books are kept in cupboards against the wall, with the journals (about fifty in number) displayed in two display units.

SERVICES

There is a functioning loan service. The library of the Lycée Technique grants home loans to a small group of readers made up mostly of teachers and administrative staff. Home loans are made for up to a fortnight. As for consultation on the spot, it can be done on all opening days. There is direct access to the collection. Visits are recorded daily in a register. Table 4.5, overleaf, gives an extract from this register.

The library receives an average of 83 readers a day, a satisfactory figure. The library of the Lycée Technique leaves a very good impression on all its visitors. Its organization, the decorations on the wall, the reception by the librarian, the relative quality of the collection are certainly enough to explain the rate of use. The room is always full and quite quiet.

USER SATISFACTION

The users of the library of the Lycée Technique already have a reading culture. The academic demands are high and mastery of

Table 4.5 Visits to the library of the Lycée Technique over a two week period

Date	No. visits	No. pupils	No. teachers	No. others
17-11-1997	83	82	1	
18-11-1997	101	98	3	
19-11-1997	84	84		
20-11-1997	143	131	8	4
21-11-1997	68	64	4	
24-11-1997	54	45	9	
25-11-1997	52	52		
26-11-1997	106	99	6	1
27-11-1997	42	42		
28-11-1997	103	100	1	2
Total	**836**	**797**	**32**	**7**

technology requires a great deal of research and hence of reading. Each day readers flock to the library and the librarian is stretched to the limit. She cannot single-handed make home loans and loans on the spot, watch the readers to make sure that they do not leave with items, process the few documents that she receives, etc. Physically, she cannot manage given the number of visitors each day (83 visitors). That is why she has long been trying to get her school management and the school authorities in general to recruit another librarian so that together they can spend more time with readers and speed up the service.

The results of a user survey show that:
- 53% are satisfied with the library's services;
- 80% claim that only by increasing and improving the collection, can the library fully meet its readers' information needs;
- 78% (the teachers in particular) desire subscriptions to journals. As the library specializes in technology, the lack of subscriptions to scientific and technological journals is a major handicap. This gap must be filled in order to achieve quality training in technology.

An interview with the Director of Studies of the Lycée revealed that four key problems are hampering the proper operation of the library:
- the smallness of the premises;
- the lack of an autonomous budget making it impossible to supply the library with items and materials on a regular basis;

- the lack of opportunity for in-service training for the librarian;
- the lack of a national policy to recruit specialist librarians.

Conclusion

In the course of this research on school libraries in Mali, four main problems were detected.

1 The lack of a budget means that the libraries are almost totally dependent on external aid and gifts of books and materials.

2 The lack of spacious and suitable premises means that all the libraries visited in this survey are contained in class-rooms. The cupboards are in most cases against the wall and the chairs are arranged in the middle of the room for readers. Readers are often inconvenienced by library business such as the stamping of new acquisitions.

3 Virtually all the librarians at the secondary level are teachers who have no training opportunities. They have attended OLP's fortnight-long course, but that course by itself is not sufficient to cover all the areas of library documentation and information techniques, especially when it is not followed by other training either within Mali or overseas.

   Moreover, the government, taking refuge behind the constraints of the International Monetary Fund, is refusing to recruit young graduates who have specialized in librarianship. That would have made it possible to strengthen the existing staff and improve the quality of library services. What happens is that the schools continue to make transfers of secretaries out of their offices and of teachers out of their classrooms to libraries. While that makes it possible to reduce the rate of recruitment of young graduates into the civil service, it creates and fosters incompetence in the manage-ment of libraries. The government seems not to understand that no speciality can replace another, if supplementary training is not given. And if that is true, why offer this supplementary training, when state-trained specialists exist?

4 The total absence of a national policy in the areas of infor-mation and documentation. Both school and public libraries have been created piecemeal. Worse still, no reliable regula-tions governing librarians have yet been adopted. It is true that there was an attempt to do so, but the result is good only for the archives. No school or university library has a set budget. Nor are there in any ministry sections respon-sible for managing, monitoring and coordinating the actions of libraries in an appropriate way.

Recommendations

In order to remedy the problems listed above, the following recommendations are made:

1 Each school library must be equipped with an autonomous budget or at least a set figure allocated to the library.

2 A library should be included in the architectural design of every future school. For existing schools, it is vital to adapt their library to a suitable architectural design.

3 The government and school authorities must do everything to ensure the further training of teacher librarians in particular and other librarians in general. Librarianship is an evolving science and librarians must not find themselves left behind by developments in data communication, etc., otherwise the conservation and diffusion of information, the springboard for socio-economic development, will suffer greatly. Channels to ensure the training and further training of librarians are not exploited. Co-operation with European universities, for example, should not be limited to courses for Malian teachers. Librarians should also have the chance to get further training in the libraries of those universities. In addition, each year, study bursaries are granted by international associations, foundations, etc. But the information does not reach the librarians who so need it. Finally, potential for training exists within the country. The Ministry could organize training courses whose animator would be a specialist from within the country or abroad. Courses in the framework of twinning arrangements should also not be forgotten. It is only by exploiting these channels that our librarians will get further training. Recruitment of young graduates for all these reasons must be a priority if we want to have professional librarianship.

4 The preparation of a national information and documentation policy whose broad lines will be: planning and creating libraries, providing libraries with an operating budget, recruiting and training of librarians, creating a national centre for the acquisition and distribution of documents, determining for each type of library a central one and, finally, book promotion.

5 Within this policy, especially at the level of the basic schools, and especially in this period of decentralization and economic constraints, there must be maximum involvement of the population. The establishment and maintenance of school libraries requires a partnership between the government and the people.

Chapter Five

CLASSROOM LIBRARIES: SOUTH AFRICA

THULI RADEBE

Background

Socio-economic and political context

Since the new dispensation of 1994, the Republic of South Africa comprises nine provinces, namely, the Western Cape, Eastern Cape, Northern Cape, Free State, KwaZulu-Natal, North West, Gauteng, Mpumalanga and Northern Province. According to preliminary estimates produced by the Central Statistical Services (CSS) in October 1996, the population of South Africa is approximately 37.9 million people. South Africa's Gross National Income, measured at average 1993–95 prices, was US$130,918 million, equivalent to US$3,160 *per capita* (Hutcheson, 1998:956).

The legacy of apartheid is that most South Africans are under-educated and under-prepared for full participation in social, economic and civic life (Krige *et al.* 1995:79). Since the new Government of National Unity came to power in 1994, a number of human rights which were denied under apartheid rule have been extended to all racial, ethnic and religious groups in the country. The country is currently undergoing a major transformation, but the deep and long-lasting damage caused by apartheid has led to numerous transition problems.

Education policies and practices

NUMBER OF SCHOOLS AND SCHOOL ENROLMENT

The Education Foundation (1997: 3) recorded 27,188 schools in the whole of South Africa, with an estimated pupil enrolment of 11,869,000 pupils (South Africa, CSS, 1997). De Villiers (1997: 80) estimated that more than 400,000 pupils annually enter the former black departments. These departments have a history of inefficiency and low pass rates and appear to lack a learning culture. Krige *et al.* (1995:79) referred to some estimates which put the number of 'out of school' children in South Africa as high as 2.5 million, with between 25% and 74% of African children in large areas of the country being out of school.

HISTORICAL OVERVIEW OF EDUCATION

Segregated and inferior education was legislated for Africans in 1953 by the Bantu Education Act, for coloureds in 1963 and for Indians in 1965, providing an ideological cornerstone for the social segregation, economic exploitation and political oppression of these groups to varying degrees, according to race (Nkomo, 1990:1). The Tricameral Parliament came into effect, alongside the homeland system, through the Republic of South Africa Constitution Act of 1983 (Kaniki, 1997:3). By the same Act of 1983, blacks in the self-governing territories outside the borders of South Africa ran their own education systems under 'own affairs'. A separate Department of Education and Training (DET) administered black education within the borders of South Africa (Kaniki, 1997:3). This dispensation spawned fifteen Ministries of Education (some sources estimate 19) in South Africa (Karlsson, Nassimbeni and Karelse 1996:6; de Villiers 1997:79). The fifteen Ministries and their Departments were differentiated along racial and ethnic lines in accordance with the apartheid system and philosophy of Christian National Education which entrenched the unequal allocation of educational resources. After the first democratic elections of 1994, a single Ministry of Education was established. The history and inequalities of South African education have been described by many writers (see Baine and Mwamwenda, 1994; de Villiers, 1997; Krige et al., 1995; Sidiropoulos, 1997).

Krige *et al.* (1995:78) set the national average pupil/teacher ratios at 41:1, whilst there are many districts in KwaZulu-Natal and the Eastern Cape with pupil/teacher ratios of more than 46:1. In the former Transkei, for instance, almost all districts have between 48 and 100 pupils per classroom, though even worse scenarios have been revealed informally by education authorities and teachers in KwaZulu-Natal, with some ratios around and in excess of 70:1. National goals in this area are 40:1 and 35:1 in primary and secondary schools respectively, to be reached by April 2000 (Sidiropoulos, 1997:197).

De Villiers (1997:80) observed that while schools played a major role in dismantling apartheid, they also helped to undermine a learning culture in South Africa. Manifestations of the breakdown in the learning culture were characterized by the late arrival of pupils and teachers, early departures, class dodging, truancy and even basking in the sun. A level of apathy in both teachers and pupils is also observable (Karlsson, 1996:8).

Fundamental Pedagogics was the theoretical foundation of educational policies in apartheid South Africa (Higgs, 1997:100). This theory was more about socialization than philosophy, and more about instilling passive acceptance of authority than providing students with the conceptual tools necessary for creative and independent thought (Taylor, 1993:3). Furthermore, Higgs (1994:90; 1997:100) concluded that Fundamental Pedagogics restrained the learner from participating critically in learning interaction, thus instilling a spirit of intolerance, and an unwillingness to accommodate divergent perspectives and points of view. This feature strongly characterizes South African political debate today.

The shortcomings of teachers, including their lack of information handling skills, have been pointed out by a number of authors (Stadler, 1992; READ, 1993; Radebe, 1994; Behrens, 1995). Some of the teachers who register for the Diploma in School Librarianship were incapable of locating and accessing information, analyzing and synthesizing this information and formulating their own opinions (Radebe, 1994:43). Most teachers confessed to a lack of confidence in their own English language proficiency (READ, 1996:19); furthermore:

> ... their professional training has not stressed the importance of reading, or equipped them to involve pupils in the learning process. (READ, 1993)

The curriculum in training colleges does not equip teachers-in-training with skills to integrate information skills with their subject teaching (Karlsson, Nassimbeni and Karelse, 1996:11).

It is argued that a new discourse is needed in South Africa to promote a philosophy of education that is open and critical, and which encourages learning, enquiry, discussion and ongoing debate (Higgs, 1997:105). Correspondingly, the *White Paper on Education and Training* (South Africa, 1995:31) stipulated that courses for teachers should equip them with skills to select and use a wide variety of resources, employ methods which cultivate independence in learning, and which demand on-going growth in reading competence. *Curriculum 2005*, the new national curriculum for the 21st century, is based on the ideal of lifelong learning for all South Africans (South Africa, 1997a). The new curriculum will effect a shift from a content-based to an outcomes-based education. One of the changes envisaged as a benefit of this change, is that learners will know how to collect, gather and organize information and conduct research (Isaacman, 1996). Access to a wide range of learning resources is a critical and essential component of the new educational paradigm and not an optional luxury (Karlsson, Nassimbeni and Karelse, 1996:13). One role of the school library within outcomes-based education is to provide learning resources for different phases and levels to meet the pace and needs of each learner (South Africa, 1997b). The discussion document on school library provision standards (South Africa, 1997b) identified the school library as a suitable vehicle to provide resources for learners and acquire basic skills. Although the new initiatives look positive on a theoretical level, the new system is plagued by the same inefficiency problems as before (de Villiers, 1997:80) because the same teachers, who lack motivation and efficiency, and the same apartheid era administrative personnel are still running the system.

Information provision

The South African library and information system is relatively well established with, in 1991: school libraries; two national libraries; three legal deposit libraries; four provincial library services with numerous affiliated public libraries; ten independent public libraries; 88 university, college and technikon libraries; 465 special libraries; 91 government department libraries; ten 'national' libraries in the previous homelands; and about 120 resource centres (National Education Policy Investigation, NEPI, 1992:7). However, a negligible number of libraries was available to black people in the apartheid era either in the townships or in rural areas. The other races all had access to public and school libraries in varying degrees but higher than blacks. Indian and coloured townships were provided with public library facilities. The homelands were each provided with a 'national' library but with insufficient funding, some less than those of urban municipal public libraries (Stadler 1992:45). It was only after 1973 that some city public libraries opened to all races (Radebe, 1996b:51). Public librarians around the country have seen an upsurge in the number of black people who are using these libraries. Many resource centres, according to Stadler (1992:45) were established during the mid–1980s by non-governmental organizations (NGOs) as an attempt to fill the gaps in information provision created by apartheid structures. Within the past three years a number of public or community libraries have been built by the KwaZulu–Natal Provincial Library Services in black townships and rural areas.

SCHOOL LIBRARY PROVISION

The various education administrative departments were different even in the way they handled library and media matters (NEPI, 1992:9-10), with a few of the departments formulating a specific library policy. The Department of Education and Training (DET), the single largest provider of schools for African learners, only officially acknowledged the role of school libraries in teaching and learning in 1983. Prior to this development, there was no legal imperative to provide school libraries or train teacher librarians for African schools, resulting in generations of African learners and adults who are library illiterates (NEPI, 1992). Krige *et al.* (1995) reported that as many as 76% of all schools in KwaZulu were without libraries. Six years later the situation had not improved with Schroen (in Karlsson, Nassimbeni and Karelse, 1996:8) estimating that only 20% of schools in KwaZulu–Natal had libraries. In Soweto, of a total of 317 schools in 1992, only 80 (25%) had school libraries (Stadler 1992:44), her further estimation being that R2.5 billion (US$587 million) would be required to provide all schools under its jurisdiction with a library.

The Education Foundation (1997:3) reported an alarming shortage of school libraries. Table 5. 1 gives the number of schools with libraries by province.

Table 5.1 Number of schools and schools with libraries in South Africa (*EduSource Data News*, 17 August 1997)

Province	No. of schools	No. of schools with libraries	% of schools with libraries
Eastern Cape	5 880	433	7%
Free State	2 881	341	12%
Gauteng	2 233	983	44%
KwaZulu–Natal	5 409	955	18%
Mpumalanga	1 907	290	15%
Northern Cape	526	175	33%
Northern	4 107	205	5%
North-west	2 412	340	14%
Western Cape	1 770	916	52%
TOTAL	**27 188**	**4 638**	**17%**

Out of a total of 27,188 schools, only 4,638 (17%) have libraries. This 17% is concentrated mostly in white and Indian schools and to a lesser extent in coloured schools. It is estimated that it would cost approximately R450,000 (US$105,634) to build one school library with an area of 300 sq.m. excluding the stock (Bawa, 1996:238).

The entire education system during the apartheid era was also characterized by, amongst other things, people in positions of authority lacking an understanding of the relevance of learning resources in libraries. The administrative inefficiencies of the DET and many other factors neutralized the impact of efforts by departments which attempted to address the deficiencies and backlogs by distributing books and other media to schools (Karlsson, Nassimbeni and Karelse, 1996:12).

The research by the National Education Policy Investigation (NEPI) into library and information services (LIS) suggested that library and information services should be governed within the framework of national educational policy with libraries integral to education at the formal and non-formal level (NEPI 1992, Walker 1993:76, 77)). The TRANSLIS Coalition, a collaboration of ten LIS groupings launched in 1992, grew out of co-operation achieved by the NEPI LIS Research Group (Stilwell, 1995). The mission of the TRANSLIS Coalition was to develop a national library and information service policy and programme. Regional branches of what is now the TRANSLIS Forum continue to work in some provinces, such as KwaZulu–Natal, towards producing policy documents which will direct the provision and governance of libraries in the provinces. Another research body, the Committee for Education Policy Document, was hired by the ANC in 1994 to further develop LIS policy and to translate policy proposals into implementation plans or strategies. This resulted in the Implementation Plan for Education and Training document which notes the central role that information and libraries play in all educational sectors (Stilwell, 1995). In its policy proposals the ANC proposed that every education and training institution would provide its learners with access to appropriate library and information services (ANC, 1995:85).

There is a policy document which provides a national policy framework for school library standards (South Africa, 1997b:3), but the nation is yet to see practical delivery. As de Villiers (1997:80) warned earlier, the inefficiencies which plagued education still characterize the department today, coupled with an immense backlog which far outweighs available finances. The attitude of the Education Department towards school libraries has also not improved. Cutbacks have targeted school libraries and the arts (Baker, 1994:141). Full-time qualified teacher-librarians have increasingly been withdrawn or given greater teaching portfolios because schools cannot afford specialist teacher-librarians when no provision has been made for them in the teacher/pupil ratio allocations (Bawa, 1996:219).

The remainder of this chapter presents an evaluation of the value and impact of the classroom library as a means of providing access to reading material at the primary level of education using the READ Educational Trust as a case study. It is not an examination of the READ programme but rather an assessment of the modality of classroom libraries. In South Africa, the READ classroom library model has been suggested as an alternative to the traditional school library (Karlsson, 1996:3).

READ Educational Trust

READ is a non-profit-making educational trust which has thirteen regional offices around the country. READ began in 1979 with a small group of volunteers and is funded by the South African private sector and foreign funding agencies. It was founded in response to community concern regarding the lack of reading and library services in black townships (Menell in READ, 1992:3, 1996:1). The mission of READ is:

> To help people throughout South Africa to develop their reading, writing, learning, information and communication skills so that they can become independent life-long learners. (READ 1996:1)

The organization has clear objectives which aim to improve and enrich the learning experiences of all learners by promoting learner-centred teaching methods in a stimulating environment, thus providing them with various essential learning skills.

The READ programme consists of practical training programmes for principals, librarians, teachers, student teachers and community workers to inculcate in learners independent learning skills and improve language competencies through the use of books and other materials; it provides library resources as well as on-going monitoring of projects to ensure that agreed objectives are met and that materials provided are used by educators and learners to improve reading and communication skills across the curriculum (Menell in READ, 1996:3).

READ has strong in-house assessment and evaluation processes which involve the teachers assessing themselves, as well as being assessed by their colleagues or principals, and by READ staff (READ 1995:5). READ courses demonstrate:

> ... the growing capacity to evaluate outcomes in the classroom with a considerable degree of accuracy and to use those evaluations both as benchmarks and as a basis for comparison with situations in which our programmes are not offered. That capacity has already demonstrated most emphatically the measurable and highly cost effective value of our programmes in the classroom. (Menell in READ, 1996:3)

READ programmes

PROGRAMMES FOR TEACHERS

- READ's **leader-teacher programme** trains teachers in core READ courses and their support materials. The leader-teachers are encouraged to share their skills in the use and making of teaching aids in workshops with colleagues in surrounding schools (READ, 1997:10).

- The **primary school programme** is a continuum of courses designed to improve the professional skills of language and subject teachers and librarians while improving the language competence and cognitive development of the children. This programme enables them to move from traditional rote learning to a child-centred, story-based approach which promotes active learning (READ, 1996:7).
- The **high school programme** involves the development of courses for teaching information skills (READ, 1996:8).
- The **partnership for change programme** is a focused series of courses in Educational Management for Change.

Opportunities for the certification of READ programmes have begun to emerge (READ, 1995:7). Teachers who have attended READ courses are offered credits by the Natal College of Education in Pietermaritzburg when they register to further their qualifications and the University of Port Elizabeth includes modules from READ courses in the diploma course offered as part of its in-service teacher training programme. The incentive of formal recognition and accreditation from the Education Department motivates teachers to apply the underlying theories and philosophies of a resource-based approach to learning English (READ, 1997:7).

MATERIALS DEVELOPMENT

- READ designs courses and materials which are inexpensive and are aimed at encouraging teachers to write new material with their pupils (READ, 1996:12). The approach follows international trends in language and literacy development. The materials are graded according to difficulty, and are not tied rigidly to particular school standards. This flexibility, in terms of level, means that it is possible to distribute the same materials to pupils of differing cultural and linguistic backgrounds, providing a way of unifying and democratizing the classroom experiences of all school-going South Africans since,

  > ... the argument that different sectors of the population require different learning materials could be seen to represent exactly the forms of cultural and racial segregation favoured by the architects of apartheid. (READ, 1995:8)

- **Big Books** contain original, previously unpublished stories for non-mother tongue English learners;
- **Picture Story Packs** contain full-colour posters, Little Books and a Teacher's Guide (READ, 1996:13). The objective is to

stimulate pupils to tell or write stories and to improve
cognitive skills;
- **Afrika-Tales** are indigenous oral tales from all over Africa
(READ, 1996:13);
- **Theme packs** enable teachers to develop language, literacy
and learning skills across the curriculum.

SPECIAL PROJECTS

READ runs a number of special projects which all support the basic
premise that reading is the key to life.
- The **Teachers' Training College project** provides a cost-effective way to assist student teachers in improving their own
reading and information skills, while at the same time introducing them to a variety of appropriate teaching strategies
(READ, 1995:7). For example, the College Librarians'
Association in KwaZulu–Natal which has developed into a
strong lobby group which has been able to tackle the
Provincial Education department on matters of policy
(READ, 1997:11).
- The **Sunshine in South Africa Pilot Project** comprises books
which are story-based and cross-curricula in content, have
been cross-referenced to the specific learning outcomes of
Curriculum 2005, and can be easily translated into other
languages.
- The **Festival of Books** (FOB) which involves dramatizations of
stories and choral verse and explores ways in which stories can
be used to develop pupils' language skills (READ, 1997:13).
- The **READathon** is a national literacy awareness campaign
(READ, 1997:13).
- As part of the IDT/ODA (now DFID) **Fifteen Schools Book
Project**, the Independent Development Trust, through a
network of eleven regional trusts, since 1991 has built
12,000 classrooms in rural and urban primary and secondary
schools all over South Africa. In support, DFID (the British
Government's Department For International Development)
funded a two-year project to supply fifteen completed
schools with libraries of UK and local books as well as
complementary training. READ selected the material and
conducted the training (READ, 1997:13).

READ's role in the new education paradigm

Various national documents on teacher training, curriculum development and a national qualifications framework are being applied
to curriculum development at provincial levels. READ already
offers in-service and pre-service training in active, child-centred

teaching methods and outcome-based learning. Increasingly READ is working with educational authorities, subject advisers and college lecturers in this regard (READ, 1996:12).

The IPET document (Centre for Education Policy Development, 1994) recommended that READ should service all the nine provinces of South Africa by offering fully designed training programmes, including the train-the-trainer programme. READ is negotiating with various education departments to use its programme to assist the implementation of *Curriculum 2005*.

Evaluation findings

A report, based on a survey of pupils participating in READ's programmes on reading and writing skills, drew a number of important conclusions (Le Roux and Schollar, 1996:18–22):

- the findings point out the dire need for attention to be paid to the reading skills of black pupils;
- READ schools are very clearly ahead of their counterparts in terms of reading and writing – the READ schools outperformed their control school counterparts by between 189% in Standard 3, 151% in Standard 4 and 104% in Standard 5. Pupils in READ schools have accelerated their language proficiency skills by up to two years. In terms of their reading scores they are ahead by 18 months whilst in terms of writing scores they are over two years ahead at the same stage (Le Roux and Schollar, 1996:20);
- there are major differences (over 60% on average) between the urban schools and the rural schools in terms of pupils' reading performance which READ (1996:18) attributes to lack of exposure of the rural farm school children to books, newspapers, magazines, television, radio and other media;
- the selection of reading materials is a vital and critical element in the process. South African children, especially those in the deep rural areas, have special needs and requirements. There needs to be a definite focus on those needs when it comes to the selection and writing of materials suitable for South African conditions;
- the role of the teacher in a book-based approach cannot be overestimated. The most successful schools visited were those with enthusiastic, motivated and committed teachers who had received good in-service training and back-up;
- READ schools participate voluntarily, without any 'formal' recognition or incentives. The incentive of formal recognition and accreditation from the relevant educational authorities, would motivate teachers to apply the underlying theories and philosophies of a book-based approach to learning English.

READ's classroom libraries

The information on classroom libraries comes from READ annual reports and a paper presented by Mrs Cynthia Hugo, the National Director, at a conference on School Learners and Libraries held in Durban, KwaZulu–Natal in November 1995.

What is a classroom library?

READ's initial classroom library provision is a selection of about 60 books, consisting of fiction appropriate to the child's reading and interest level, non-fiction closely related to topics on the curriculum, and a few reference books such as dictionaries and an atlas. These resources are placed in a strong, lockable, portable wooden box which functions both as a storage container and a display cabinet. Story-board and poster materials have also been designed to be used together with the classroom collections. READ has developed and run training programmes for schools in which their boxes are placed (Hugo, 1996:89). Usually the collection is on loan to the teacher and materials have to be returned and replenished each term or each month, in order to meet the new curriculum needs of the learners and the teacher (South Africa, 1997b:35). The materials are required to be kept in the classroom and kept accessible for easy use by pupils. READ has successfully piloted this model in many schools across South Africa. A READ classroom library, as estimated during the NEPI policy exercise, cost R1,335.50 (US$313.50) in 1995, excluding training and delivery costs, with about 15 boxes being required per primary school (Bawa, 1996:239). Thus the cost per school, excluding training and delivery costs, would be in the region of R20,032.50 (US$4,702.50).

The purposes or objectives of READ's classroom libraries are:
- to provide learning resources for teachers coupled with training programmes to show the teacher how to use books to make content lesson teaching more interesting;
- to provide resources for learners to use;
- to enable teachers to move away from the 'tyranny' of textbooks and demonstrate to learners that facts can come from more than one source;
- to enable teachers to demonstrate to learners how knowledge is selected, presented and interpreted in different sources thus leading learners to develop critical thinking and appraisal skills;
- to prepare learners for visits to a central school library or community library through being introduced to book organization and classification, which are essential skills to their future independent study and research skills;

- to ensure that a reading culture flourishes;
- to add colour and a centre of interest to the classroom (Hugo, 1996:89).

How classroom libraries are used

Children are first encouraged to use the classroom library by choosing their books for the silent reading lesson. Later, learners are allowed to handle the books freely and they are encouraged to read books in free periods. Children are encouraged to take books home and share them with other members of the family when they have learned proper care of books. The classroom library also helps teachers introduce learners to finding and using books on reading for information.

Why the classroom library?

READ noted the bleakness of many classrooms and how the teachers' ability to teach creatively was severely hampered by a lack of resources as well as a need for more professional training (READ, 1994:3). Such classrooms could not become 'sites for learning' and reliance on the textbook alone would continue the practice of rote-learning and teaching. The poor classroom is char-acterized by a lack of books, teaching aids, visual stimulus; rote learning; a teacher who lacks confidence; pupils who need greater stimulation; and an atmosphere of rigid discipline (Hugo in READ, 1994:10). It thus became READ's aim to transform as many class-rooms as they could into the 'READ classroom' where teacher and pupils have the best possible opportunity to make education a posi-tive experience. The classroom transformation begins with the box library.

Most South African children come from homes where very little reading takes place, where there are no books and a reading culture is not understood. A weak book culture and lack of reading in the home has a negative effect on the whole of a child's learning. Introducing children to an intimate and pleasurable knowledge of books can be facilitated by providing classroom libraries in all classes and by training every primary school teacher to introduce pupils to books as an integral part of their learning and leisure experience. The presence of book resources within the classroom means that books and book-related learning are integrated into the learner's classroom experience from the first grade. Learner-centred teaching and independent learning relies on an adequate supply of appropriate resources. Reliance on the textbook and rote learning is more likely to continue to be common practice where there is a lack of such resources (Hugo, 1996:87-90).

Perhaps the greatest strength and advantage of this model is the close and constant proximity that learners have throughout the school day to a set of appropriate learning resources. Further, although the school is not able to build up and invest in its own library collection, educators and learners benefit by having access to a collection which is constantly replenished with the very latest publications and productions, selected by professional staff. Another great advantage is that implementation of this library model does not require the school to have a post for a professional teacher-librarian. Instead, one teacher performs a co-ordinating role and the other teachers attend in-service training on how to use the classroom library effectively (South Africa,, 1997b:36). This is most important at a time in South Africa when posts for teacher-librarians are being taken away and given to teachers or when teacher-librarians are being given full or heavy teaching loads (Bawa, 1996).

Arguments against classroom libraries

Arguments against classroom libraries and in support of the central library are that:
- it makes for economic use of resources;
- it provides a wider range of materials for pupils to select from and therefore, in theory, improves their skills in selecting relevant information;
- it teaches pupils to use a large collection (as compared to a classroom library), which is important if they are to use secondary school and other libraries competently later on;
- it provides a quiet study area – this is one of the library's functions although it should not be its main one (Gibbs, 1985:310).

The discussion document (South Africa,, 1997b:35) based occasional negative perceptions of the classroom model on the fact that because the classroom library was only offered in African schools, it was perceived to be a cheap compromise in providing African learners with some half-hearted form of library provision.

Methodology

Choice of methodology and rationale

The method used to collect data for this study was the focus group discussion. The strength of this method lies in providing an opportunity for probing and clarification. The mailed questionnaire method would have been expensive and unreliable. The timing of the study coincided with school examinations, a time that is not suitable for involving teachers in additional activities. However, not more than two hours a day was required for the study and this resulted in a very good response rate.

Sample

Although the READ classroom libraries function around the whole of South Africa, the study focused on three districts within the Pietermaritzburg Region of KwaZulu–Natal Province. This was due to cost as well as time constraints. The three districts surveyed in the study are the Midlands, Pietermaritzburg and Umvoti Districts, as designated by the Provincial Education Department.

The population of the study was primary school teachers who were running classroom libraries and who had been trained, irrespective of the level of grade they taught. Three leader-teachers (one from each district) were also interviewed, separately from the teachers, on their experiences. This was because, whilst they are leader-teachers, they are also running their own classroom libraries. The three library advisers (one from each of the three districts) also provided information through letters on their experiences, especially relating to the training of teachers and principals and on their experiences at the schools. In total, 29 teachers from all three regions participated in the group discussions, giving a 73% response. The 29 teachers who participated (7, 9, and 13 from each of the three districts) were all from schools which had functioning libraries. Those from schools where the classroom libraries were not put to maximum use did not come to the discussions.

Data collection and analysis

A semi-structured interview framework was used in the pilot study and adapted accordingly thereafter. The first section of the framework was aimed at addressing the issue of provision and availability. The second section addressed relevance including materials selection, the curriculum, sufficiency of numbers of books and type of materials. The third section addressed the issue of staff training, including follow-up sessions. The fourth section addressed impact, which covered independence in accessing of library, independence in selecting materials, inculcation of analytical and critical thinking skills (deciphering and challenging of differing viewpoints, formulating their own arguments and drawing conclusions) and reading skills. This limited the number of questions to 21. Group discussions lasted for an hour and a half to an hour and three quarters each (Day, 1993:390).

The intention was to collect both qualitative and quantitative data but since there was always an overwhelming agreement on issues, quantity was not an issue (no need for frequency counts). The researcher regarded differing on an issue from the groups by one or two people as 'rare event' data and did not report on it unless the comment was of particular importance (Widdows, Hensler and Wyncott, 1991:355). The group's responses were summarized to determine the extent of agreement.

After all the discussions, the researcher did a contents analysis after organizing the data by topic and editing them in sequential order until broad themes emerged (see Kamfer, 1989:8 and Widdows, Hensler and Wyncott, 1991:355).

Problems

The first limitation in the present study was that only the 'good' teachers turned up for the discussions, although that in itself confirmed a problem which was raised by all participants, namely, a lack of commitment by many teachers.

The aim of the study was to evaluate classroom libraries for effectiveness and cost effectiveness. Effectiveness of classroom libraries is not a straightforward phenomenon and it was difficult to measure in this study. No single measure of effectiveness is sufficient to describe an organization. Secondly, no single definition of organizational effectiveness will suffice (Van House and Childers, 1993:1). In this study, trying to establish in practical reality the best approach and the best indicators for measuring effectiveness of classroom libraries was no easy matter!

Measuring cost effectiveness was another difficulty. To address this indicator, the researcher has commented on her observations and reported on comments relating to cost effectiveness made in the literature as well as by READ staff.

Findings

In this section teachers who participated in the discussions are referred to as participants, whereas leader-teachers and library advisers are referred to as such.

Availability of materials

SIZE AND SUFFICIENCY

All participants agreed that at the time of the survey their libraries contained more than the 60 items that had originally been supplied; in some instances they were double the original size. This was because, although they were allowed to exchange libraries with READ, these libraries were in fact never returned to the organization. READ had a level of flexibility which enabled it to deal with schools on an individual basis. Instead, the classroom library had been increased through additions, with exchanges only between classes within the same schools. The average class size was around 35 (up to 40); in eight cases two classes shared a room, resulting in a class size of 70.

The general feeling was that the original 60 items had been sufficient for the number of pupils. When two participants from one district expressed a need for duplication of non-fiction titles, other participants reminded them that the non-fiction in the classroom libraries was not meant to replace textbooks. (A number of people have argued against the use of any library as a storeroom for textbooks.)

Size of a collection cannot alone determine its quality, as it says nothing about the content or condition of the items (Doll, 1997:95). The age of the collection is one possible measure of quality. Since READ materials are curriculum-based, are produced by READ themselves in response to identified needs and their programmes are reportedly ahead of *Curriculum 2005*, good quality is assured. Facilities to replenish or enlarge the library are easily available – it is a matter of a telephone call to the adviser and if available the materials are delivered. Participants reported that the decision to enlarge or exchange the collection is an internal school's arrangement. Once a pack has been exhausted they are permitted to exchange for different ones if necessary.

Although the participants and leader-teachers were generally happy with the materials, they expressed a need for more and different books around the middle of the year. They all agreed that the need for more was not a reflection of insufficiency on the part of the READ library but rather a reflection of 'greed for more' on their part and that of the pupils. One of the participants stated that, 'as with anything one enjoys in life, one starts noticing and hunting for more books'. They claimed that READ has trained them to be active, and instilled an inquisitiveness in them which makes them always look for more, which they are also fostering in their pupils.

NEED TO ACCESS OTHER COLLECTIONS

To satisfy this 'greed' and generally to support the curriculum, participants expressed the need to access other libraries. The necessity for teachers to access information sources from beyond the school is well supported in the literature. Kuhlthau identifies access to outside sources through technology as one of the elements of success in the implementation of the process approach to information skills (1993:16). A consultant for READ suggested that local libraries should be requested to make available copies of the recommended books as a further source of information for students (Brindley, 1991:60).

All participants agreed that the classroom library was not sufficient for teaching all library skills to both pupils and teachers. Some claimed that what was lacking was experience of a big library as well as exposure to the 'technical' side of library procedures. To solve this problem, six participants who teach in Pietermaritzburg have entered into a formal arrangement with the Natal Society Public Library. According to them this is because READ has trained them to be enterprising and to network. Through this arrangement the teachers occasionally take pupils to the library to do block borrowings and take the materials back to their schools to enrich their classroom libraries. At the public library the pupils are put through the mundane library procedure of registering, getting cards, selecting materials and taking them out, for instance. By this time they are already acquainted with the organization and classification of the materials in their classroom libraries and thus understand the sequence and the purpose of the bigger library.

One group suggested exchanges of books between schools was a way of accessing other collections. This is because their relationships with READ started at different times and therefore makes some of them 'old' and others 'new'. The general feeling was that both groups would benefit from such exchanges: the 'old' schools would send their old books to the 'new' schools which would then get to enjoy those books which might be regarded as 'classics', the 'old' schools would get access to new books as they often envy the 'new' schools when they receive new and more attractive materials.

All participants expressed a need for replenishing their collections on a yearly basis. This would require support of the education department to address the problem of funding.

Accessibility of materials

OPENING HOURS

Apart from one school, which only allowed pupils to access the classroom library once a week, the rest said there were no restrictions – it all depended on the situation in each class. The only restrictions are those instituted in order to maintain some order especially where schools were running combined classes in one room, at the same time.

Some participants reported how they had combined a number of classroom libraries into one central library, but also continued to run their classroom libraries. Each class spends a formal library period in the central library once a week, with free access to the classroom libraries. On Fridays everyone is free to visit the central library. Pupils are also free to access libraries before school assembly, during breaks and after school to encourage them to regard a visit to the library as a leisure activity like any play activity. Teachers had concluded that free access was rewarding to the child and some had trained the pupils to 'grab a book when idle' and that 'the best friend you can ever have is a book'. Some had made bookmarks out of those slogans. This corresponds with Baker's report (1994:136) of a teacher at Walter Teka School in Greater Cape Town (a READ school), who has also created a central library by putting all the books from the Grade 7 boxes into her classroom, making it both a English subject specialist room and a place where children can read whenever they have a chance. There was no formal system for borrowing books, but children could take books home by arrangement with the teacher.

The general observation from the participants was that the teacher's role and attitude to the library was crucial in maximizing access.

LOANS

One school reported that it did not allow pupils to take books home for fear of them being damaged. But all the other participants agreed that, initially, pupils were allowed one item at a time but that it depended on the individual pupil's reading speed and performance.

All participants and leader-teachers reported that Friday is a special day on which pupils are allowed to take out as many books as possible depending on availability. This is when fast readers tend to be restricted by having to wait for books to be returned. It had become normal practice for teachers in such situations to borrow from other classes, especially from those whose books 'lie covered in dust', when they ran out of materials for fast readers. This is done in an attempt to avoid holding back those pupils. In one school they also borrow from higher classes for higher functioning pupils, and they encourage pupils to use the local community library or the public library in town.

Baker (1994:136) also observed that there are schools in Cape Town who work with READ where books remain inside their boxes, hardly touched. One of the reasons for this is teachers' anxiety about children losing or spoiling the books. She also reported on keen readers in the class who go through the books that interest them quickly.

All the participants who allow pupils to take books home reported that they have stopped allowing this for pupils in Grades 1 and 2. From their experiences they have found that from Grade 3 pupils are able to look after the books responsibly at home. This must be seen in the light of majority of parents in the rural areas being illiterate and not being confident with books. This appears further to confirm teachers' anxiety, referred to by Baker, about books getting lost or spoilt.

All the participants reported that they had been trained to devise their own ways of controlling the stock. Some used cards originally supplied by the Department of Education and Training until they ran out and then started devising their own system. The majority of schools had simply prepared record books in which pupils record their own issues and returns. In some cases, class library monitors are also trained to monitor the situation.

From their observations, the participants concluded that the learners were satisfied with the amount of time they were allowed with the books. A lot of flexibility was reported in a number of situations, which allowed teachers to respond to individual needs in terms of time. According to participants and leader-teachers, learners plead for extensions of time with the books – the more the pupils get acquainted with reading the more they want – they can never have enough!

Training of teachers

The national training workshop for leader-teachers is run every year by READ trainers at READ headquarters. The training of teachers is done by the leader-teachers locally under the supervision of, and with, the library advisers as a team.

All leader-teachers and participants reported a flexibility in organizing in-service teacher training sessions, they provide as many sessions as are needed and as it is possible to provide – sometimes it is simply a matter of a telephone call to the adviser or a meeting to solve a problem.

Support of principals

Support from the top for READ's training workshops was reported as crucial. All participants, backed by library advisers, agreed that the biggest problem was lack of support from principals or head-teachers. Where principals are supportive things tend to go more smoothly. If a teacher from a school where the principal is not supportive is away attending a workshop, the class might have to stay away from school. In some instances principals insist on teachers taking a day's leave to attend a workshop or some training. In some farm schools, problems are posed by farm managers who do not understand the occasional absence of teachers from school to attend workshops for the benefit of the pupils. Teachers are often forced to fund their own travelling costs to get to workshops (a problem when they live far from town), because many principals believe that the training is for the teacher's own gain.

One library adviser reported that some of the teachers who are most reluctant to allow learners the freedom to use books are the men teaching higher primary classes, often they are the school principal.

Kuhlthau identified that one of underlying principle for success of the project was for the principal to show interest in the project. In her study, the assistant principal of the school gave the project credence by making formal observations of teachers and the library media specialist as they worked with students, and by talking to students about their work he showed the importance of the project. The administrators provided the climate for teaming, the time for planning, and promoted, recognized and rewarded those involved (Kuhlthau, 1993:16). This was in line with Gibbs' assertion (1985:310) that in any school it is crucial to have the support of the headteacher if the library is to be seen as important.

At the same time, the participants and leader-teachers admitted that in some instances the principal is used as a scapegoat and the teachers are in fact the culprits. Leader-teachers reported frustration at teachers' passivity, which the participants equated with a negative attitude held by some of their colleagues.

Interpersonal relations

READ library advisers were commended by all participants and leader-teachers for their acknowledgement of teachers' innovations and suggestions and for treating them with respect and dignity. Co-operating with READ was always rewarding, according to all participants and leader-teachers. The fact that travelling costs are borne by individual teachers confirms their commitment and co-operation and indicates trust between READ and teachers in their common goal, that is, excellence for pupils.

Training problems

All participants agreed that there were no problems with training from the side of READ. Participants from one district reported sometimes experiencing problems with implementation of what had been learnt. They added that sometimes they were given too many goals and less specific objectives to be achieved. The leader-teacher, however, reported that the number of objectives was sufficient but problems arose out of some teachers' inconsistency in attending follow-up workshops and sessions where many objectives are clarified.

Follow-up workshops can be invaluable for effective professional development since they help give clear frameworks, practical examples of alternative classroom approaches and follow-through which involves help given after initial training, through informal channels and through the creation of specific opportunities for discussion, evaluation and the sharing of problems (Markless, 1986:22).

Leader-teachers and participants complained that many teachers resist new teaching methods and are set in teacher-centred teaching and in perpetuating rote learning. Library advisers reported that, whilst individual teachers have been converted to the success of getting their pupils 'hooked' on reading and use of books and drama as an important part of classroom activity, other teachers in the same school might have reservations about departing from traditional, more prescriptive methods of teaching and use classroom libraries with reluctance and occasionally hardly at all. This, according to leader-teachers, results in precious materials remaining covered in dust from lack of use.

Classroom libraries and the education system

At every READ workshop, the objectives of classroom libraries are identified, explained and used as guidelines and linked to the skills that the libraries are aimed at inculcating. At the end of every session, there is evaluation to establish whether or not they have been achieved. This is a very strong element in the successful running of classroom libraries.

The participants and leader-teachers agreed with library advisers that there is no conflict between the objectives of classroom libraries and those of the Department of Education. In the old dispensation, participants and leader-teachers reported that they had experienced a conflict when the education department emphasized written work and completion of the syllabus, whereas READ emphasized reading and speaking. READ's philosophy corresponds well with outcomes-based education (OBE) and its flexible approach to the changes in education allow it to fully support the new OBE and *Curriculum 2005*. Participants and leader-teachers concluded that READ's classroom library objectives have always been clear, enriching (aimed at giving the child independence in many skills) and are complementary to those of the Education Department.

Full support from the national Department of Education was reported by all participants and leader-teachers, with encouragement and invitations to extend READ's work into more schools, which financial constraints have made difficult, however.

User satisfaction

SELECTION OF MATERIALS

Materials' selection is done by the READ library advisers, a process in which teachers are not involved. A few participants from two districts felt that they should be involved in the selection as they understand the pupils and are the ones working with the libraries. The majority disagreed, reminding the complainants that they could not really expect to be brought into the process because READ was only helping out, and READ's selectors were trained to do this specialized job, furthermore, it was easy for them to send materials back if they were not satisfied with their relevance. Leader-teachers explained that READ does involve them by seeking their advice on the issue.

Although READ does publish its own books, library advisers are led in their selection by attractiveness and appeal to the various age groups, not by country of publication or publisher. Classroom libraries contain both local and imported books.

RELEVANCE – NON-FICTION

The non-fiction materials, which participants viewed as a valuable asset in their libraries, support theme-teaching across the curriculum. In some instances teachers do not need to use set text-books because the non-fiction in the class libraries is very good and relevant, that being ensured by the fact that READ develops its own non-fiction to support various subjects. The materials are more interesting to use than the set textbooks because they are colourful and up to date and appropriate to levels.

Participants indicated that the number of copies provided poses a problem where a book serves the purpose of a textbook. To address that problem, many teachers have established relations with previously advantaged schools in the city who have made their duplicating facilities available to them. Again, recognition should go to READ for equipping them with networking and enterprising skills.

RELEVANCE – FICTION

READ's selection policy has been in many ways a policy of redress, in terms of both supplying books to the deprived, and in terms of trying to choose books that are relevant to the lives of black children. Selectors tried to move away from the Eurocentric books often found in South African schools generally. They sought out books with black characters and local settings (Baker, 1994:136). However, participants from all three groups reported that they themselves had reduced the number of books depicting the rural African context because they found that pupils displayed no more interest in them than in those with European and American contexts. Therefore, focusing on books with rural African settings was not necessary even for rural children. The participants' argument was that rural children would not necessarily live out their lives as rural adults. They further argued that rural children would attend tertiary institutions with urban children and would not enjoy being treated at that level as a special species that has not been exposed, through books, to a variety of situations.

Participants also emphasized that for South African children it is important to include white people, Indians, towns, town houses, mud houses, the beach, etc., because they all form part of the South African environment. Participants and leader-teachers claimed that sometimes books about white people are approved of by the pupils and enjoyed more than those which supposedly represent black people.

The participants and leader-teachers felt strongly about the issue of westernization. Their general feeling was that black people, like other races, cannot run away from westernization. Neither can they reject westernization because that is the way they have lived since they were born, without necessarily avoiding their traditions. One stated that, 'a so-called western way of life is the only way many of us know and that does not mean that we are rejecting African traditions. We are surviving in the world not only in South Africa'.

Other writers have written about the danger of restricting the background of fiction to what is known. Brindley concluded, in a research projects into black students' reading preferences, that whether the book is written by a black writer is less important than whether the story is enjoyable, relevant and easy to understand (Brindley, 1991:59). Baker warned that in attempting to find relevant local books, selectors may be offering a narrower range than children want, claiming that texts are multi-voiced, and can appeal to different children on different levels.

Perhaps as a result of and in response to all this research on pupils' reading needs and preferences, READ appears to be moving away from their earlier selection policy of favouring books with black characters and local settings and moving to the provision of books with mixed settings.

Pupils' satisfaction

Participants agreed that pupils were satisfied with the materials. Both fiction and non-fiction were thoroughly enjoyed by pupils, especially the fiction and other genres such as drama, choral verse and rhymes, which the participants and leader-teachers claim are valuable for teaching language skills. The reported involvement resulted in improvement in their reading, learning and writing skills, in presentation, vocabulary, expression and in the confidence and the sense of achievement and pride pupils display when they do well. Of all the fiction in the classroom libraries, picture books are the most popular materials especially for younger pupils because of their attractive colours and illustrations.

Support in running classroom libraries

Participants reported that READ's help and support is 'just a telephone call away'. Support is also available from colleagues – more recognition of READ nurturing the team spirit.

Impact on pupil skills

Participants and teacher-leaders asserted that each teacher's creativity and ability to manipulate materials to support each subject is crucial in the use of the classroom library. This is in addition to the commitment, performance, activeness and liveliness of the teacher. In one participant's words, 'the size, richness and use of the library by pupils reflects the amount of work the teacher puts in'. They emphasized that the role played by the teacher determines the extent to which children enjoy and make use of library materials, insisting that it is easy for the teacher to destroy the love of reading and other skills or to stunt their development. Furthermore, they stressed the important role played by each pupils' individual cognitive capabilities in the successful attainment of skills.They acknowledged that each child is an individual whose individual interests, values, capabilities and needs have to be taken into account.

- **Independence in accessing the library** All participants and leader-teachers explained that children take different time spans, but in general participants estimated that within a week pupils begin to frequent the library depending on the teacher's encouragement. In addition, the time pupils take to access the library independently depends on the previous class – if the previous teacher is not interested, the pupils get to the next level without the inclination to access the library. If the pupils were motivated in the previous class, the next teacher simply needs to nurture what has been instilled.
- **Reading** All participants and teacher-leaders agreed that reading is a skill which is basic to others. The level and the pace with which this skill is developed, impacts on all the other skills discussed in this chapter. Participants claimed that improvement in reading was noticeable from level to level.

- **Selecting fiction independently** According to all participants, this is the easiest skill for the pupils to grasp, although again, the teacher's direction and encouragement is crucial.
- **Using reference materials** All participants and leader-teachers concluded that at the beginning pupils need a lot of supervision and encouragement in using reference materials, especially to choose from the right levels. If the teacher does not give supervision and guidance, a pupil tends to grab whatever catches their eye. Teachers' commitment, depth of knowledge and activeness are important attributes.

  All participants and leader-teachers declared that READ's reference books are good as they are colourful and contain pictures which makes it possible even for Grade 1 pupils to start using them independently from about three weeks.
- **Critical thinking skills** All participants and leader-teachers agreed that the improvement in these skills is really notice-able. From Grades 2 or 3 pupils display these skills depending on the teacher input. The estimation was that it took about seven months, at any level, from the beginning of the year for the teacher to see the change in these skills.

  Two districts mentioned that pupils do their own book evaluations. Many participants agreed that it was rewarding to hear pupils discussing the cover of the book and many different views emerging. Pupils start challenging and criti-cizing one another and are able to draw their own conclu-sions and formulate their own arguments. The pupils get used to reading critically. This confirmed Brindley's sugges-tion (1991:60) of stressing to students that they are the eval-uators and their opinions matter even when they differ from those of the teacher.
- **Deciphering and formulating viewpoints** All participants claimed that by the time pupils get to Grade 3 they can deci-pher differing viewpoints and can formulate their own, adding that it really depends on the teacher and individual capability of the child. For instance, if something the pupils have been taught is presented differently on television they challenge the teacher on it the next day. This means that they can get information from different media and they can relate this to what they were taught.

Continuity between classes

One of the greatest concerns expressed by all participants is the lack of continuity between classes. One teacher's diligence can be easily nullified by the teacher at the next level who is not committed to the skills which have been instilled at the previous level. Factors responsible for this lack of continuity, as raised by the participants and leader-teachers are discussed below.

- Many principals are not committed to READ programmes, do not go for training and so do not insist on making READ workshop attendance and library use compulsory. The lack of support by a number of principals was also said by a library adviser to be the biggest problem leading to failures in programme implementation. Another library adviser stated that the schools which implement READ's methods to the best advantage are the schools with involved principals who work with their teachers as a team and who formulate a library policy for the whole school. As she put it, 'the odd reluctant teacher in these circumstances is usually carried along on the wave of peer pressure and is forced to make extra effort'. Participants and leader-teachers also raised the problem of unqualified teachers who are never sent on courses.

  Ray's suggestion (1994:8), that the introduction of a whole-school policy for information skills would solve many of the problems such as lack of support from head and teaching colleagues, is worth taking seriously. All participants argued that a school-based monitoring system is necessary to maintain a high standard of consistency amongst teachers. This system would be useful for motivating teachers to stay on track and to support training for new teachers and also to run refresher courses for those who have been working with class libraries for some time.

  Participants, leader-teachers and library advisers suggested that READ should canvas as many principals as possible, since they have a lot of success with those who are already genuinely involved. They agreed that the chances of success in this area would be strengthened by the Education Department declaring the READ programmes compulsory for all teachers and principals.

- One library adviser reported that staff changes, especially if a supportive teacher or principal is replaced with a non-supportive one, adversely affect continuity. Leadership problems in a school were reported by all in the study as damaging to continuity in the running of classroom libraries.

- Lack of funding is the other factor which affects continuity. Already library advisers and leader-teachers have reported that, due to lack of funds, it was no longer possible to provide materials. One library adviser reported several requests from schools new to her circuit, who have seen READ libraries and teachers' and pupils' work, but who they will not be able to take on unless they get more funding.

Cost-effectiveness

READ is audited frequently with detailed financial statements being made available to the stakeholders, the public and funders. Although it has not been all plain sailing, READ has had regular funders for many years, funding would probably not have continued if donors were not convinced of the cost-effectiveness of READ's classroom libraries and supporting programmes.

Pupils in READ schools have accelerated their language proficiency skills by up to two years. In financial terms, this must surely reflect one of the best returns on investment in all education funding and spending (Le Roux and Schollar, 1996:24). This was confirmed by the observation made by all participants and leader-teachers that pupils from READ schools, formerly and still mainly black, do not struggle to get into mixed schools in the city where entry and admission is preceded by an interview. A number of instances were cited in which READ pupils have not been held back in terms of entry level as is 'normally' the case for pupils from previously disadvantaged schools. These comments confirm the value of the classroom libraries and the programmes which accompany them.

Parental involvement

Parental involvement is a strong feature of the READ programmes and the Trust emphasizes it at all levels as part of teachers' professional development. It is READ's philosophy that the reading habit cannot be sustained with success without parental involvement, since it is an activity to be enjoyed by all. The premise is that the more parents are integrated into the life of the school, the better it is for their children's education, particularly with regard to reading (READ, 1997:8). Teachers requested that READ include literacy classes for parents in its programme. Parents are encouraged to read with their children, to ensure and confirm that learners have read the books they claim to have read and to attend various reading festivals and other related events (READ, 1994:6).

However, the country has to face the fact that the majority of parents are illiterate so their involvement in their children's education can be a problem. For instance, the participants from urban schools reported that they had a measure of success, whereas those from rural schools advised that the parents needed a lot of counseling. An inferiority complex, arising from illiteracy, reportedly played a role in countering genuine involvement of these parents. As the participants asserted, this issue of parental apathy requires further in-depth investigation, if solutions are to be found.

Additional suggestions

Participants made a number of other suggestions, all on the understanding that the national, provincial and local education authorities would pledge full support for the READ programmes:

- **Certification** Participants would like certification after a
  number of training sessions; this would be an incentive for
  all teachers to become involved, especially as the certificates
  would be useful in career progression. Consequently one
  would assume that such certification would be recognized
  by education authorities and rewarded. Since READ is
  already issuing performance certificates which secure
  teachers credits from the Natal College of Education (NCE),
  a further suggestion was for the certification to be linked to
  and recognized by the Department of Education.
- **Festival of books** More than one READ Festival of Books (at
  least twice a year), where everyone is allowed to make a
  presentation and everyone could be a winner, was requested.
  Such a festival would be crucial in enhancing the stakeholders' commitment, many of whom do attend these occasions. The popularity of festivals was confirmed by a library
  adviser who reported an attendance of around 80% of
  teachers from the schools she used to work in at the Festival
  of Books. This also reflects on the popularity of reading,
  choral verse and drama in the schools.
- **High schools** Participants wanted READ to be more active
  in high schools to ensure continuity. Again, this requires full
  support by the Department of Education.

Conclusion

The findings of this survey on the effectiveness of classroom
libraries (as run by READ) within the context of South African
education are positive. The classroom library has benefited the
education of pupils as well the teachers' performance. It has
effected a resource-based education by enriching the learner's
learning experience in a stimulating environment. The conclusion
is that READ has the infrastructure and expertise to take South
Africa through the transformation period with their classroom
libraries.

Achievements of the READ classroom library

The classroom library provides the pupils and teachers with sufficient curriculum-based materials relevant to their teaching and
learning needs. Teachers have been allowed to accumulate and

keep materials. Their aim is to effect learner-centred learning practices and outcomes-based education. The materials allow grading according to difficulty which is a break with an absurd tradition, adhered to by the apartheid education system, to retard the black child by regarding all children as the same with the same capabilities and interests and as operating at the same level of development. The attractiveness of READ materials have transformed otherwise bleak classrooms into stimulating environments conducive to positive learning experiences. What is more, the location of the books in the classroom makes them easily accessible at all times of day, both by the teacher and the pupil.

Although READ's practice of using only their staff, whom they have trained and exposed to a variety of views in the selection of materials for the classroom library, was criticized by some of the participants in the focus group discussions, it works well. To select books, one must have an in-depth knowledge in the field; leader-teachers are involved in selection and their views are always considered. They have been trained in the area and are able to make a contribution which includes teachers' recommendations. Although READ have tended to favour books with black characters and local settings against Eurocentric books, the teachers are allowed to send back what they are not impressed with, as they pointed out in the discussion. And READ do now offer a mix in terms of settings and contexts in their books; they are not restricted exclusively to black and rural settings. This change reflects READ's ability to respond to requests and suggestions from teachers and to reports on pupil preferences.

One finding of the survey is that the role and input of the teacher is absolutely crucial to the success of the classroom library. A major strength is the integration of teacher training into the READ programme. This has enabled teachers to move away from the tyranny of textbooks, instilling in them the view that knowledge comes from a variety of sources and that there is always more than one view on an issue; it has equipped teachers with critical thinking and information handling skills which the colleges of education have not inculcated in them and which are essential for the successful running of a classroom library. READ training thus makes up for the inadequate curricula in colleges of education. The evaluation and assessment component which is built into READ courses and materials is a valuable tool which provides a mechanism for redesigning and rewriting courses and materials. In this way teachers are never stuck with unusable and irrelevant materials. Follow-up workshops are also a strong feature of READ programmes. Another finding of the survey was that the support of a school principal is crucial. READ has recognized this and has started training programmes in this area.

Once a classroom library is in place, teachers continue to be offered support by READ through their local library advisers. The good interpersonal relations between the READ advisers and the teachers was noted as having a positive impact on the running of the library and keeping teachers committed to the programme.

The classroom library does not limit users in their search for information. Instead it has proved to be a stepping stone to the use of a larger library. It is important to note that the enterprising spirit instilled in teachers by READ, has made teachers take it upon themselves to forge relations with other libraries for the purposes, amongst others, of exposing pupils to more 'technical' library skills and of nurturing their classroom libraries. The findings of the survey also show that classroom libraries have succeeded in inculcating confidence in reading, materials selection skills, and analytical and critical thinking skills in pupils.

The classroom library as a model for the future

In this present climate of 'no funds' for providing each school with a library and a teacher-librarian to run it, READ's classroom library appears to be a most appropriate model. It does not require the school to have a post for a teacher-librarian. Instead, every teacher trained by READ can run a classroom-based library. And the cost of training teachers in classroom library skills is much less than that required for training teacher-librarians. It has been pointed out that at the moment 22,500 schools in South Africa lack libraries.It costs on average R450,000 (US$105,634) to provide each school with a library, excluding stock compared with R20,032.50 (US$4,702.50) which is required to equip a school with a set of 15 classroom libraries. Planners and decision makers will need to consider this if a solution to the lack of library resources is found in time for the implementation of the new curriculum. The final objective of a library for every school can still be maintained, as it has become evident that it is possible to build a central library from classroom libraries.

Regarding cost-effectiveness, although we have a sense of the cost of classroom libraries, this survey has found it difficult to relate that cost to their effectiveness. At the same time we have the evidence that pupils in READ schools have accelerated their language proficiency skills by up to two years and are very clearly ahead of their counterparts in the control schools in terms of both reading and writing. In a simplistic way, the present researcher concludes that these resources are indeed cost-effective, especially as the funders remain loyal after a number of years.

The Centre for Education Policy Development in 1994 recommended that READ should service all nine provinces of South

Africa. Certainly their programmes are totally in accord with Department of Education's *Curriculum 2005*. In addition, the READ programme and its materials provide a tool for assessing the specific outcomes outlined by the Department of Education, making it possible to identify performance criteria. READ has focused on schools in rural areas, where problems are more extreme and entrenched by greater poverty, geographical and political isolation, fewer employment options, feelings of dependency exacerbated by more bureaucracy and traditional authoritarianism and resistance to change. The national, provincial and local departments of education can learn a lot from READ regarding ways of bringing rural schools on board.

Unfortunately READ does not have an endless supply of funds to extend their resources to every school and every teacher. This already causes problems in continuity from class to class and from school to school. Support is now needed from the Department of Education. For example, developing a whole-school policy on the compulsory use of classroom libraries will have to have the full support of the Department. The issue of parental involvement in rural schools is still one to be addressed. This is a complex area which requires the involvement of the Department of Education. A lot of research is needed to address issues such as the suggested counsell ing to deal with deep-rooted problems of an inferiority self-concept, apathy and general non-involvement of parents in their children's education. Where adult literacy projects are in place, some improvement is witnessed. Most of all, direct financial support from the Department is required if READ is to extend its programmes on the scale needed.

BOOK BOX LIBRARIES: MOZAMBIQUE
WANDA DO AMARAL

Background

Socio-economic and political context

Situated on the south-eastern coast of the African continent and bordering the Indian Ocean, Mozambique plays an important role for a group of countries in southern Africa (Malawi, Zambia, Zimbabwe, Swaziland and the South African province of Gauteng) by offering an outlet to the sea.

Although the majority of the African population was originally 'Bantu', which in turn encompasses several distinct ethnic groupings, there are also minority groupings of Asiatic and European origin. For historical and political reasons associated with the heterogeneity of the African languages, Portuguese was adopted as the official language. In 1990, the population was officially estimated at 15,656 million inhabitants and the estimate for 1996 was about 18 million.

Having been a Portuguese colony for almost five centuries, Mozambique, led by FRELIMO (the Front for the Liberation of Mozambique), became independent on 25 June 1975 after ten years of armed fighting against colonial domination. In the following year, with the insurgence of a political opposition movement (RENAMO), there began a period of guerrilla warfare and internal fighting, which finally came to an end in 1992 with the signing of a peace agreement. The single-party government of FRELIMO, which was initially markedly Marxist-Leninist in character, has undergone changes and since the end of 1990 there has been a multi-party democracy and a market economy.

The economic policy of the Portuguese colonial administration in Mozambique was directed towards absolute dependence on South Africa and Southern Rhodesia (now Zimbabwe). The economy was basically run to offer rail and port services, the provision of a labour force and huge plantations for cultivating tropical products for export.

After Independence, the inherited economic and social structures were completely distorted. The country had to make wide-ranging and profound changes in all areas, but in the period 1975 to 1985, this work was made more difficult by a number of factors which destroyed much of the existing socio-economic infrastructure:

- the large-scale sudden exodus of almost all the Portuguese companies, managers and technical personnel;
- armed aggression from the regimes in Southern Rhodesia and South Africa;
- internal armed fighting between the party in power and the opposition;
- a systematic and prolonged series of natural disasters (drought, floods, cyclones).

One of the biggest problems which held back attempts at major restructuring of the economy was the lack of qualified managers. This lack was caused by the frighteningly high level of illiteracy; at the time of Independence, more than 93% of the population was illiterate; currently the level of illiteracy stands at around 72%. With the ending of the war in 1992 and with a *per capita* income estimated at US$97, Mozambique was considered one of the poorest countries in the world. It embarked on the process of development by investigating a whole range of economic activities designed to allow a potentially rich country to make progress.

Educational policies and practices

The current National System of Education (SNE) began to be implemented in 1983 and has three main objectives:

- eradication of illiteracy;
- introduction of a compulsory schooling system;
- training of managers for the country's socio-economic development needs.

The National System of Education is divided into five sub-systems:

- general education;
- adult education;
- technical and professional education;
- teacher training;
- higher education;

and is structured into four levels:

- primary;
- secondary;
- further;
- higher.

The general education sub-system covers primary, secondary and pre-university education:

- **primary** education, from the ages of 6 to 12, covers first grade (years 1 to 5) and second grade (years 6 and 7);
- **secondary** education, from the ages of 13 to 15, covers 3 years (years 8 to 10);
- **pre-university** education, from the ages of 16 to 17, covers 2 years (years 11 and 12).

The structure for controlling and providing educational support to teachers, which was partially destroyed during the war and then by changes of minister and modifications to the central directives from the Ministry, is, at provincial level, made up of educational support commissions (CAPs) consisting of delegates for each subject whose role is to solve educational problems which have arisen in the schools; and at district level by zones of educational influence (ZIPs) – an ensemble of schools grouped by geographic proximity, one of which is the coordinator, whose role is to solve any educational problems which might arise.

After Independence, state investment in this sector concentrated on building schools and on implementing literacy and adult education campaigns. The civil war, which devastated the country for years, was responsible for the destruction of part of the school network which then existed. Between 1983 and 1987, at primary and secondary education level, 6,062 existing schools were destroyed and 2,677 closed, representing 44% of this network; 456,534 pupils were affected in the two levels of education in question. Table 6.1, overleaf, shows the numbers of students registered in public schools/educational institutions in Mozambique over the fifteen year period from 1980 to 1995.

Private education, which was abolished in 1975, became officially accepted again following measures adopted in 1990 and now there are several such schools from primary to higher level.

Information provision

The economic constraints which resulted from the long period of fighting and natural disasters are reflected in the very poor state and services of the documentation and information systems found in the country. In the majority of cases, the lack of financial resources and the shortage of qualified staff are the main reasons why library and information services have not developed.

The National Library, which is the responsibility of the Ministry of Culture, Youth and Sport, has no financial resources and few qualified staff and acts more as a public library for general reading than as an organization for controlling and safeguarding the heritage of publications by and about the country.

Table 6.1 Number of students and number of schools/institutions, 1980 to 1995

Levels		1980		1985		1990		1995	
		Students	Schools /Inst.	Students	Schools /Inst.	Students	Schools /Inst.	Students	Schools /Inst.
Primary	PE1	1 387 192	5,370	1 311 014	4 616	1 260 218	3 441	1 415 428	4 241
	PE2	79 899	99	111 283	156	116 718	169	127 294	234
Secondary		9 729	19	21 623	41	25 280	39	34 464	50
Pre-university		413	2	2 162	5	3 343	5	4 110	10
Tech. & Prof.	Elem.	2 807	13	747	10	98	1	158	2
	Basic	9 897	19	9 334	24	7 987	24	11 968	23
	Middle	1 047	3	1 562	4	1 847	6	2 404	11
Higher education		836	1	1 442	1	3 715	3	6 186	3

The eleven existing provincial libraries (which are also the responsibility of the Ministry of Culture, Youth and Sport) are in practice the public libraries for the provincial capitals. All these libraries are operating with greater or lesser degrees of difficulty and in most cases with the support of foreign NGOs, support which translates into the purchase of books, subscriptions to periodicals, the provision of some mobile support, financing for study visits to neighbouring countries, participation in regional conferences, etc. Some of the 128 existing districts do have libraries but the number of these is unknown.

The three existing public institutions for higher education are served by libraries but they all suffer from the same problems:

- lack of technically qualified staff;
- shortage of storage space;
- the small number of sitting areas in reading rooms;
- the almost complete non-existence of photocopying facilities;
- the non-existence of a national budget for purchasing books, which has resulted in almost total dependency on international co-operation.

Most of the ministries, national organizations and central agencies of state and government have specialized libraries/documentation centres. They have developed in very diverse ways; whereas some are already using the new technologies to provide the most up to date information, others simply fulfil the passive role of safeguarding collections of tied-up bundles of documents whose content is out of date and irrelevant.

The Mozambique Historic Archive forms part of the support structure for studying archival documents and is one of the best libraries on the history of Mozambique and southern Africa, welcoming within its walls pre-university students.

Set up as a planning activity under a co-ordination unit at central level, the School Libraries Service is the responsibility of the Ministry of Education (MINED); it was set up in 1979 but to date no policy has been defined for its development. As it is without the financial or human resources it needs to function properly, the school libraries service is almost non-existent in primary education; it operates extremely badly in secondary and pre-university schools, even where there is a library. Various projects are being carried out with the objective of awakening interest in books and in reading, principally at primary level, although these projects are not being organized by MINED but by foreign organizations.

Book box libraries

Since 1982 there have been some projects in schools in Mozambique using book box libraries, including:

- Projects where the basic objective is the improvement of the teaching/learning process, with the provision of educational materials emerging as one of the supports in this process:
  - The *mobile* libraries project which was the full responsibility (concept, finance and management) of the Ministry of Education (MINED) and embraced all primary schools in the country. (Pre-university schools have also received books from MINED, but not in the form of *mobile* book box libraries.) This project operated from 1982 to 1984 and constitutes one of the case studies examined in this chapter.
  - The *moveable* libraries project (packed in metal boxes) which formed part of an educational support programme 'Creating the habit of reading' operated by the French NGO Action Nord Sud in five districts of the province of Inhambane, covering 70 schools at primary level. Twelve boxes, each containing a collection of 59 titles (subjects: Portuguese, mathematics, natural sciences and children's literature), circulated around 70 schools, staying in each school for one month. Although these libraries continue to circulate, the project was cut back in 1996 because, starting in 1997, the NGO planned to locate a fixed library in each of the schools covered by the project. According to the manager of the project, it will not be sustainable to continue the programme of circulating libraries in the future, because the provincial and district education authorities do not have the human resources or materials (principally the transport network) necessary for maintaining access once the boxes are handed over to the government.
- Projects in which the fundamental objective is the creation of a more effective reading environment either in school or locally:
  - The *portable* libraries were part of a project supported by the Canadian Organization for Development through Education (CODE) and was carried out between 1990 and 1995, involving all primary schools (about 550) in the province of Cabo Delgado. (As there were only five secondary schools in Cabo Delgado, they were also included in the scheme.) This project constitutes the other case study examined in this chapter.

The end result of all the projects referred to above was that there was improved access to reading materials for the school population involved. However, from interviews with the people in charge of these projects, it is clear that the exchange of information about the work involved in each of these projects was not undertaken satisfactorily. Lessons learnt in one project were not transferred to the next.

Since the central coordinating agency, the School Libraries Department of MINED, does not have a strong structure, the funding agencies prefer to give support at local level to the geographic areas in which they work rather than to the system or network of school libraries, since it barely exists.

Aims and objectives

For the *mobile* libraries (Ministry of Education), the beneficiaries were the school population throughout the country aged between six and twelve years: the future teachers of primary education. The objectives were to develop pupils' habit of reading and the development of a teaching body. Factors critical to the success of the project included:

- the choice of titles being put into the collection;
- the quality of the co-ordination between the central agency (School Libraries Co-ordination Commission) and the link people for education at provincial and district level;
- planning for the circulation of the libraries;
- training for the people in charge of the libraries and their use.

For the *portable* libraries (CODE), the beneficiaries were the school population aged between six and twelve years and the teachers in the primary schools in the province of Cabo Delgado. The objectives were to provide culturally appropriate supplementary reading materials and thus to reinforce post-literacy habits by developing the habit of reading at the level of primary education. Factors critical to the success of the project included:

- the choice of titles to make up the libraries;
- the training programmes in the use of complementary reading:
  - training at director level (district education directors, directors of zones of educational influence (ZIPs), school heads); their contribution was important to the project objectives being achieved;
  - empowerment of the teachers and technical staff in the Provincial Education Service through seminars lasting one week.

MOBILE LIBRARIES

The mobile libraries pilot project was designed and managed by the School Libraries Co-ordination Commission Agency (now known as the School Libraries Department), an agency which at Ministry of Education level superintends all the problems relating to libraries.

The renewed outbreak of war, which resulted in part of the school network being destroyed, along with many of the roads, meant that this project lasted for little more than two years (1982–1984). At the time, the static school library was practically non-existent as an instrument of educational support. The impossibility of providing a library to each primary school in the country (in 1980 there were about 5,830 schools at this level with about 1.5 million pupils), led to taking up the option of the circulating book box library. With about 3,015 book boxes of three different types (years 1 to 4, urban schools; years 1 to 4 rural schools and years 5 to 6), it was possible, using a termly rotation system, to allow access to books for almost all primary schools in the country. The decision to pack these libraries in strong cardboard boxes was linked to the fact that many of the schools in the country, because they were operating under the cover of trees or in very precarious buildings, did not have the physical space to house the collection; in such cases, the boxes were the responsibility of the head of the school, who kept them in his or her own house. The forward plans for the project provided for updating and improving the collections and a gradual hand-over of the libraries to those schools which showed that they were able to set up the structure for housing them.

In the course of the project, three evaluation seminars were conducted which brought together all the people in charge of the whole project, including some of the people who formed a link with the provincial directors of education. The archives which contained almost all the documentation produced about this project have now been destroyed; all the information for this survey was collected in the course of interviews with the then head of the School Libraries Co-ordination Commission.

PORTABLE LIBRARIES

In 1990, CODE identified Cabo Delgado as the area in which to concentrate its activities. This was a province which had been very little affected by the civil war and 70% of its school network was still operating. The project, which lasted for five years (1990–1995), was the responsibility of the Cabo Delgado Provincial Director of Education and was managed entirely by Progresso, a Mozambique NGO which has the general social objective of contributing to the development of basic communities, with particular attention to women and children, and aims to raise the living conditions of the population and improve their abilities to manage themselves.

Although Portuguese is the official language and the language of instruction in schools in Mozambique, the reality is that it is a second language and there is a huge need to reinforce people's ability to understand and speak the official language of the country. This could be made easier by introducing supplementary reading material at primary school level. It is becoming increasingly clear that success in introducing these supplementary reading materials is linked to training primary school teachers in how to develop a better reading environment in their schools and communities.

The books for the libraries were purchased in Maputo by Progresso and sent to the Provincial Director of Education in Cabo Delgado; there they were packed in boxes made of material produced locally and sent off to the district education officers who in their turn despatched them to the schools. This project differed from that of MINED, in that the boxes did not circulate but remained in the school to which they were sent.

Initially, the plan was for the project to make up libraries which each contained 150 volumes (15 titles and 10 copies of each title). However, 46 titles were purchased (over a period), making a final purchase total of 166,663 volumes.

In 1993 the project underwent a positive intermediate evaluation, in the course of which it was established that one of the principal reasons why the all the planned objectives had not been achieved was the poor ability of the primary school teachers to teach the early stages of reading. The positive results of this evaluation led to approval being given for a new project called 'Improving the teaching of reading' in which, whilst maintaining the activities of the first project, there was an emphasis on a component for training teachers in the use of the book box libraries to develop the oral tradition and the ability to tell stories in Portuguese and improve the methods of teaching reading and writing to years 1 and 2.

Functions

The *mobile* libraries had the function of supporting the teaching/learning process at primary education level in all schools in the country and of training teachers at this level, by supplying books covering the teaching areas and reading books for children and young people. The function of the *portable* libraries was to reinforce post-literacy habits in the province of Cabo Delgado by developing the habit of reading at primary school level.

Governance

The *mobile* libraries project was conceived and managed centrally by the School Libraries Co-ordination Commission and operated wholly from a national budget. The choice of books and the organization of the libraries was entirely the responsibility of the co-ordinating agency. The latter then sent them, together with a list of the contents, to the provincial authority using the educational support commissions (CAPs) as the links. These people were responsible for all the activities relating to the libraries; they organized the despatch of the libraries to the ZIPs who in turn sent them on to the schools.

According to the information given during this research, there was not a great deal of understanding at central co-ordination level of how to go about receiving/despatching the libraries in the CAP-ZIP-school circuit. In the schools, the head was the person responsible for the use of the libraries and for receiving/despatching them. When the project was first implemented and in accordance with the norm which became established, the libraries for years 1 to 4 were to stay in each school for one month; requests from several schools meant that the period in which they did stay was extended to three months, which is what had already been established from the beginning for the libraries for years 5 and 6.

The *portable* libraries was a project which was conceived and presented to CODE by the Provincial Director of Education for Cabo Delgado. The role of co-ordinator and manager for the project was awarded to the Mozambique NGO Progresso which operated it in close co-operation with members of the Provincial Administration of Cabo Delgado, who were specifically allocated to the work. It was executed at province level. The Provincial Director of Education received the books, put together the libraries and sent them to the district authorities; they were in charge of delivering them to the schools within their jurisdiction.

Target user populations

The *mobile* libraries covered the whole of the school population in the country at primary education level, corresponding to around 1.4 million students in about 5,800 schools. The *portable* libraries covered the whole of the school population at primary education level in the province of Cabo Delgado, involving around 110,000 pupils and about 2,500 teachers in about 550 schools.

Methodology

Choice of methodology and rationale

The methodology used to gather data on the *mobile* libraries for this survey, because of the problems which have been identified already, was basically a series of interviews with the person responsible for the project and the use of the few pieces of archive material and reports which had not been destroyed.

The methodology was similar for the *portable* libraries. A series of interviews were held with the executive secretary of the NGO Progresso and a number of its reports and archive documents studied.

Methods used in data collection and analysis

Statistics, published annual reports and archive material from the institutions responsible for the book box libraries were used to collect background information. Written reports and other documentation were a particularly important source of information on the CODE project.

Based on the general picture which was given to this researcher in the initial interviews and after a first analysis of some of the archive reports and documents, the bulk of the data was collected through structured interviews with the people in charge of the projects. These interviews were designed to take account of the data necessary for presenting the case studies but which did not figure in the documentation used or where a reading of the same gave rise to doubts over its interpretation.

Interviews with a sample of teachers or students to gather data on satisfaction and impact did not prove possible. In the case of the Ministry of Education project, the situation of instability and mobility among the population (in this case of teachers and heads of schools) caused by the war, together with the destruction of the archives relating to the project, meant that any sampling procedure would be impracticable.

An intermediate evaluation of the CODE project was conducted at the end of 1993, based on a sample of schools in Cabo Delgado. It did not use probability sampling, which is typical in statistics, but rather 'convenience sampling', which is characteristic of qualitative methods, namely selecting elements which will supply information which is pertinent to an in-depth study. Two districts in the Province were chosen from among the first where the project was implemented, or where there was ease of access. Using the processes of interviews and direct observation, ten schools in the two districts were visited, and about 25 pupils, teachers, the people

101 responsible for the libraries, executives from the Provincial

Education Office in Cabo Delgado and the district authorities for Pemba and Montepuez who were involved in education were interviewed. The data collected in this evaluation is used in the present case study.

Problems

In respect of the Ministry of Education project, there were two significant problems. Firstly the project archives had all been destroyed (a result of changes to the structures and management organs of the Ministry); secondly the huge level of mobility among heads and teachers of schools throughout the whole country (mainly as a result of the war) meant that there was no possibility of interviewing any of the teachers or heads who had taken part in the pilot project.

Time and expense contributed to the difficulties encountered in collecting data on the CODE project. The lack of information in circulation in Mozambique on this project meant that it was only at the end of November 1997 that this researcher learnt of the existence of the project. The school teaching year in Mozambique is from February to November, which meant no data from the field could be collected until the following year, outside the time limits of the research. In addition, the costs of travelling and staying in Cabo Delgado (a province in the extreme north of the country), amounted to US$1,200, also outside the research, in terms of the funding available.

Findings

Collection development

AVAILABILITY

In both these projects, the libraries are book collections packed in boxes and handed over to the responsibility of the head of a school (MINED) or of a teacher who has been trained for the work (CODE) and potentially access is easy. However, as people were not used to 'having books' and because there was fear of losing them, the pupils' use of them and the possibility of more pupils reading them was restricted. This not being used to 'having books' also existed amongst the teachers, which meant that they had little desire to encourage the use of the libraries by their pupils.

In the case of the *portable* libraries, there were indications that in some schools the books were difficult to access for a variety of reasons:

- the transfer of the active teacher (the only one capable of managing the library) meant that the book box libraries were locked up in a room which was difficult to access;

- the person in charge of the library was a teacher who also taught during the teaching periods; this meant that no attention was given to pupils in the other lessons;
- the concept of the book box library (a wooden box containing books which was in the care of the teacher designated for the purpose of managing it and to which all the pupils must have access) had not been properly assimilated by the heads of the schools and the teachers responsible. This meant that the books were held on to so that pupils could not damage them and, for the same reason, the books were not lent out, the pupils being obliged to read them in school. It should also be noted that the school timetables did not have any periods specifically for the use of the library.

SUFFICIENCY

In the two projects analyzed, the number of titles in a box proved to be insufficient to cover need, when the number of users is considered.

In the *mobile* libraries, there was only one copy of each title in a box and the number of books in each box ranged from 31 to 76, as can be seen in Table 6.2.

Table 6.2 Number of books in different levels of mobile libraries		
Level		No. of books per box
Years 1 – 4	Boxes for urban schools	31
	Boxes for rural schools	35
Years 5 – 6		76

In the *portable* libraries, each library was made up of 15 titles and there were 10 copies of each title, making a total of 150 volumes. If we consider that 166,663 volumes were purchased to serve 106,465 pupils, this means there were 1.5 volumes per pupil, which is obviously insufficient. There were signs that in some schools the number of books was insufficient to meet the demand and the interested pupils had to wait a long time before being able to read the most sought-after titles.

RELEVANCE

In both projects, the collections were chosen with care, the opinions of specialists and educational experts were sought and account was taken of the different objectives of each of the projects.

In the *mobile* libraries and mainly in the collections which were destined for level 1 (years 1–4), the subjects were almost exclusively school subjects for supporting the education provided (Portuguese, mathematics, natural sciences). Care was again taken in putting together different collections, depending on whether the schools were located in a rural or an urban environment. The collections destined for years 5–6 included a good percentage (about 40%) of children's and young people's literature.

The *portable* libraries were made up for the most part of children's and young people's literature, with a small proportion of books being for the teaching of Portuguese (1.5%) and natural sciences (5.5%). The indicators to which this researcher had access show that the imported books were more in demand than those produced nationally, due to the print quality (mainly the colour).

SELECTION/ACQUISITION

In both cases, selection was handled by the people in charge of the projects after they had heard the views of teachers and educational experts.

For the *mobile* libraries, the books were all purchased in Portugal and then imported.

For the *portable* libraries, in year 1 of the project (covering the schools in three districts), the books were all imported from Brazil (about 14,000 volumes); in year 2 of the project (covering the schools in three districts) and in year 3 of the project (covering the schools in two districts), the books were partly imported (about 25,500 volumes) and partly produced locally (about 49,400 volumes); in year 4 (covering the schools in four districts), there was a small percentage of books imported from Portugal (about 2,550 volumes) and the great majority were acquired from local production (about 24,800 items); in year 5 (covering the schools in five districts) it was not necessary to import as they were acquired from local production (around 21,350 items) and they benefited from a UNICEF offer of around 30,000 volumes. In total, the books purchased, whether locally or imported, represented 83% of the total in the collections, the rest were donated.

ORGANIZATION

The libraries were packed in boxes, either cardboard or wood. The small number of the books meant that the contents were easily visible and no organization such as classification or cataloguing proved necessary.

Staffing

For the *mobile* libraries, the coordinating agency for this project had a sector head, with a degree in history and philosophy, who worked closely from 1979–1981 with a Cuban national who was a specialist in school libraries; the coordinating agency also had three education experts who had basic training in documentation. During the First National Meeting of School Libraries, held in 1982, it was agreed that at least one person from each of the provincial education authorities (qualified with a degree in education) and answering to them should act in the province as trainers of the teachers and heads responsible for the libraries in the schools; a small guidebook on the organization and management of school libraries was prepared and distributed at that time. It is felt today that this preparation was insufficient because, in most cases, these 'trainers' did not pass on the knowledge they had acquired and did not circulate the guidebook.

One of the objectives of the *portable* libraries project was 'to develop and carry out training programmes for teachers in primary schools in the use of supplementary reading material'. Throughout the five years of the project, a total of 729 teachers and education staff were trained in annual seminars which lasted a week and which were run by a team of provincial trainers, which stayed together for the five years. The seminars provided minimal training in the organization and management of this type of library and were accompanied by the distribution of a short guide.

Physical facilities

An advantage of the book box library is that it does not require physical facilities such as buildings, table and chairs or shelving. In both the MINED and CODE projects, the libraries were often used under the trees, which is where even today some schools in the country operate. These libraries do not need a specific building in which to be kept, it is the responsibility of the head or the teacher to keep them in his or her home outside school hours.

Finance

Due to the destruction of the archives, there is very little financial data available in relation to the Ministry of Education (MINED) project. Financing was wholly the responsibility of MINED via the general state budget. Table 6.3 gives the costs of the books (i.e. their cover price only). It should be noted that there is no record of the costs of customs charges, packaging (boxes), transport, training, seminars, management, etc.

The *portable* libraries project, which covered about 550 schools was wholly financed by the Canadian organization CODE, which contributed 544,432 Canadian dollars. The costs of the project over the five years are given in Table 6.4.

Both projects were financed centrally, one by central govern-

Table 6.3 Mobile libraries: cost of books in US$

Level	No. of libraries	Cost of books per library (US$)	Total cost (US$)
Years			
1 – 4 Boxes for urban schools	1 511	41	61 951
Boxes for rural schools	1 714	27	46 278
Years 5 – 6	102	191	19 482
Total	**3 327**		**127 711**

Table 6.4 Portable libraries: cost of service in US$

	1990/91	1991/92	1992/93	1993/94	1994/95	Total
Physical resources (boxes and recovery of one library)			2 379	17 529	4 500	24 408
Development of human resources (training)	11 240	32 020	11 892	16 307	13 018	84 477
Purchase of books	4 973	7 000	23 994	34 434	27 018	97 419
Evaluation		763		8 381	153	9 297
Management (Progresso and Prov. Ed. Auth.)	6 263	14 298	14 468	16 129	16 294	67 452
Local production of books	3 755	14 732	1 541	36		20 064
Total	**26 231**	**68 813**	**54 274**	**92 816**	**60 983**	**303 117**

ment and one by a funding agency. There were no local financial inputs, whether at the province, school or user level.

Use

For the *mobile* libraries, the destruction of the archives and the fact that the project was a long time ago, meant that little could be discovered about usage. Because there were insufficient checks by the coordinating agency, there was little statistical data on the use of the libraries available at central level. Moreover, there was no form of training on how to use the libraries given either to teachers or to school students.

Documents to which this researcher had access show that the Progresso NGO tried to obtain statistical data on use of the *portable* libraries by sampling two districts and three libraries in each of them. The three libraries in the Montepuez district did have papers which were more or less complete. This was quite unlike the three libraries in the Pemba district where, because few statistical data were supplied, no opinion could be formed. One can only conclude that no statistical record was kept in these libraries in relation to the use of the books, notwithstanding the fact that there was an exercise book in each box for recording loans and checking them.

In the statistical sample from the three schools in the Montepuez district, over a period of one year, each of the students visited their respective library 0.33, 1.3 and 1.4 times; in respect of the loan service, the number of loans per student per year was 0.9, 1.1 and 1.3. On the other hand this low level of usage must be weighed against the finding that in some schools, given the small number of books, there were waiting lists for the books which were most in demand.

The evaluation of the *portable* libraries project also found some cases where, because the teachers and heads did not encourage or facilitate the use of books either by teachers or pupils, the use of the libraries was little more than a vain hope, in terms of both reading in school and home loans.

The population covered by both projects, in most cases, did not have access to any other sources of information, which was the basic reason for creating these libraries in the first place. It could not access supplementary reading material through any other means.

Evaluation

Costs and cost effectiveness

For the MINED project, the only data which existed related to the purchase price of the books, is shown in Table 6.3. However, by adding to the purchase price estimated % costs of packaging and transport (25%), customs duties (5%) and indirect costs (15%), it is possible to arrive at total costs for the 3,327 libraries acquired. These are given in Table 6.5.

Therefore, given that about 1,349,000 students were served at level 1 of primary education and 95,600 at level 2, over the two year period of the project's operation:

- the cost of the service per school student at level 1 was US$0.12;
- the cost of the service per school student at level 2 was US$2; and:
- the average cost of a book box for level 1 was US$51;
- the cost of a book box for level 2 was US$288.

Table 6.5 Mobile libraries: total costs of service

Level		Cost per book box (US$)	Total cost US$)
Years 1 – 4	Boxes for urban schools	61.87	93 486
	Boxes for rural schools	40.76	69 863
Years 5 – 6		288.30	29 407
Total			**192 756**

For the CODE project, Table 6.6 gives the number of book boxes provided against the total cost of the service.

Table 6.6 Portable libraries: number of boxes provided and cost of service

Year	No. of book boxes	Total cost of service (US$)
1990/91	100	26 231
1991/92	117	68 813
1992/93	115	54 274
1993/94	115	92 816
1994/95	128	60 983
Total	**575**	**303 117**

Therefore, given that about 110,000 students were served in 550 schools, over the five year period of the project's operation:
- the cost of the service per school student was US$2.75;
- the average cost of a book box was US$527.

These costs are low. To be able to provide access to supplementary reading materials at an average of around US$3 per student over a five year period is negligible compared to the overall costs of education. However, the question must be asked as to how effective the access provided was. It did not prove possible for either project to conduct interviews with users, so it is difficult to make any evaluation in relation to the level of user satisfaction achieved. But the data acquired during the evaluation of the *portable* libraries project may act as indicators in this matter:
- the fact that people are not used to having books and the fear of losing them restricted free circulation of the books among the pupils;

- 'in many schools the library is almost a secret between one or two teachers';
- in some schools, the books were insufficient to meet the demand, giving rise to long waiting lists for getting hold of a title a person wanted to read;
- the 4-colour books which had good graphics were the most sought after;
- some of the locally produced books were not much sought after because the texts were long and sometimes difficult;
- the fact that there was just one active person per school who was also a teacher during lesson time meant that the pupils in other lessons were ignored.

In short, access to the collections was not easy and once accessed there was an insufficient number of books, some of which were not very relevant to need. However, and in relation to the level of user satisfaction, the following may be maintained: the almost total lack of knowledge among the population about books, libraries and how to use them led these users to be very undemanding in terms of the quality of the services provided for them.

Overall, based on the experiences of the two projects, this modality can be judged effective: the costs were low, yet some access to reading materials was provided to a large target population who had never before had any sort of information provision. Both projects constituted a first and unique experience in the provision of access to information.

Impact

For the MINED project, there is little available data on whether the provision of the *mobile* libraries improved educational performance or the quality of education. In the various interviews which were conducted with the people in charge of the project, it was maintained that in the three evaluation seminars which were held during the two years, some teachers and heads had affirmed that as a result of using the libraries, their schools suffered fewer repetitions and saw school performances improved.

As for the *portable* libraries, the results from the sampling carried out during the intermediate evaluation showed that, mainly due to the poor teaching abilities of the teachers of pupils in the early years, the educational benefits of the libraries on the teaching of reading and writing was not satisfactory. According to the final report on the project, 'the only ones who liked reading were those who could read', 'to promote the taste for and habit of reading among children, their own teachers must know how to *read* and cultivate this taste for reading'.

Conclusion

Overall assessment

Considering:
- the non-existence of access to information of the school population (primary education) in the country;
- the economic impossibility of providing a library for each school;
- the need to complement the teaching/learning process by the use of a library;

the book box library is a possible and cost-effective solution. It provides the school population with books, the basic tools for creating the habit of reading. The person in charge of the MINED pilot project states that it was a success and that it proved the viability of this kind of access to information. The benefits of the CODE project were obvious in the province of Cabo Delgado.

The main weakness of the *mobile* book box lies in the need to ensure that the libraries circulate properly and in the need for a functioning transport network. The later experience with the French NGO Action Nord Sud project, which has already been mentioned, confirms that any lack of sustainability of this type of project in the future lies in the missing transport network and in the lack of functioning infrastructures at provincial and district education level.

The biggest weakness of the *portable* libraries project seems to rest in the teachers' lack of preparation and the non-existence of a methodology for teaching reading and writing.

In both of the projects described, preparation of the managers of this type of library proved to be insufficient both in terms of the quality of training and in terms of the numbers of people trained.

Future prospects for book box libraries

Mobile book box libraries cannot be considered as a sustainable modality in the short or medium term because of the poor educational and communications infrastructure. In order to be viable and sustainable, the modality of the mobile book box library presupposes the existence of strong co-ordination at all levels (central and local) and a good transport network or nothing will come of it.

Portable book box libraries, which have already been tried out in two provinces of the country with the support of the Canadian CODE organization, seems to offer a safe solution for providing access to information for the school population when, *inter alia*, the following are taken into account:

- the existence of many schools which operate in precarious conditions, for example under trees (mainly in the rural areas);
- the fact that improving the country's educational system, which is already under way, is a long process which requires economic and human resources which are not fully available.

The modality of the portable library, in boxes, introduced a new library concept (wooden box containing books which are in the care of teachers who are trained for the work and to which all pupils have access); under this concept, the library is moveable, portable, simple, produced locally and may be acquired at low cost.

The success of this modality depends in large measure on the ability of the active teachers who are responsible for the libraries, their ability to use a methodology for teaching reading and writing and to assimilate and apply the new library concept, because those teachers who are not used to 'having books' find it difficult to provide access to them for the pupils.

With positive experience of seven years of activity which has already covered two provinces in the country, it is up to someone of the stature of the Minister of Education to study and analyze the strengths and weaknesses of this experience, starting with this evaluation, and to design a project which can be phased in to cover all the provinces. Particular attention should be paid to rural areas where the school population does not have any other form of access to information and to those schools which do not have the conditions necessary for housing a conventional type of library.

Chapter Seven

TEACHERS ADVISORY CENTRES: KENYA
CEPHAS ODINI

Background

Socio-economic and political context

Kenya achieved Independence in 1963 after a protracted struggle during which the indigenous people regained self-determination and control of their destiny from the British colonial administration. Kenya's population increased from 5.4 million in 1948 to 16.1 million in 1979 (Kenya, Central Bureau of Statistics, 1995). The population is currently estimated at 27 million and the population growth rate in the urban areas is more than 7% per annum. The population of Nairobi, the capital city, has increased from 897,000 in 1980 to approximately 2 million in 1997. This increase can be attributed in large part to rural-urban migration. Kenya is characterized by a young population – almost 50% of Kenya's population is less than 15 years of age (Kenya, National Council for Population and Development, 1994).

In Kenya, agriculture remains the leading sector in stimulating economic growth. Although the government has played an important role in the economy, private enterprise has been given more weight in the development process and today accounts for about two-thirds of the gross domestic product (GDP).The economy's performance has tended to elicit two types of response. There are those who have admired Kenya's economic achievements terming them as 'remarkable', especially when considered against the general background of other African countries. There are others, however, who have regarded the country's economic record since Independence as superficial, arguing that its experience gives a good example of 'economic growth' without 'economic development', where the benefits from growth do not reach the really poor target groups (Ikiara, 1988).

In spite of the upswings and downswings that the Kenyan economy has undergone in the post-Independence era, its performance can be said to have been generally impressive. GDP in real terms has grown fairly strongly, for example, real GDP increased almost threefold between 1964 and 1984 from K£715 million to K£1,900 million. The gross investment, wage employment, government expenditure and revenues and other indicators all show immense expansion of macro-economic variables during the period.

Educational policies and practices

The government has continued to invest heavily in education since it believes that education and training are important ingredients for creation of the manpower required for all aspects of national development. In addition to government contributions, Kenyans have joined hands in the true spirit of self-help ('harambee') to build and maintain physical facilities in schools and colleges for the education and training of their children.

After Independence in 1963, it was clear that the education system inherited from the colonial era did not meet the social, political and economic needs of independent Kenya. The first post-Independence Kenya Education Commission, under the chairmanship of Professor Ominde, was set up in 1964 to review the whole of Kenya's education system and has influenced and guided national policy for education ever since.

Subsequent reviews of the educational system in areas of structure and curriculum, (Ndegwa, 1971; Gachathi, 1976; Mackay, 1981; Kariithi, 1983; and the Presidential Working Party on Education and Manpower Training for the Next Decade and Beyond, 1988) testify to the important role that education and training continue to play in nation building.

The Mackay Report of 1981 recommended changes in the structure of education from the former 7-4-2-3 to an 8-4-4 system, which was implemented in phases starting with primary education in 1985. The 8-4-4 system is a three-tiered system composed of a free eight-year primary cycle followed by a four-year secondary school cycle and a four-year university education or other skills training programmes. It offers a practically-oriented curriculum and has introduced technical and vocational skills leading to a wide range of employment opportunities.

Although formal pre-school education is a relatively new development in Kenya, it has already become a firmly established sector of the national education system. Since Independence, there has been a rapid growth of pre-primary schools which mainly cater for the three to six year-old age group. There are approximately 18,000 pre-primary schools catering for 900,000 children in the country.

Primary education is, however, regarded as the basic cycle of the national education system. The programme lasts eight years, from ages six to fourteen, and aims at providing functional and practical education to the majority of children who terminate formal education at the end of the cycle. At the same time, primary school education caters for those wishing to continue their schooling into the secondary phase.

Primary education in Kenya is universal and free but not compulsory. The government took definite steps towards universal primary education through the abolition of school fees for Standards I to IV in 1974 and for the rest of the primary classes in 1979. However, due to the very high growth in population coupled with rising financial responsibilities, the government has adopted a 'cost-sharing policy' to facilitate the provision of basic education for all.

The post-Independence expansion of primary education is reflected in the increase in the number of children enrolled in schools, the number of teachers and the number of schools. The enrolment has increased from 892,000 in 1963 to about seven million in 1997. Similarly, the number of teachers has increased from 23,000 to 185,000 while schools have increased from 6,000 to 14,000 in the same period. However, there is a wide regional variation in the participation rate of children aged between six and fourteen years in primary education. Low enrolment is found mainly in the semi-arid and pastoral districts.

The 8-4-4 system of education reduced the time allocated to the secondary education programme from six to four years and expanded the curriculum to include applied subjects. There has been a very rapid increase in the number of schools and enrolments since Independence. In 1963 there were only 151 secondary schools with a total enrolment of 31,120 pupils. In 1997 the total number of schools had risen to 3,500 and the enrolment to 700,000 students.

Secondary schools fall under three major categories. Firstly, there are schools which are fully financed and maintained by the government. Secondly, there are those which are sponsored by communities or religious bodies but receive government assistance in the form of teachers and sometimes some financial support in form of grants. The third category is the unaided schools. In this group the majority are community 'harambee' (self-help) schools which do not receive any form of government assistance and private schools which are established and run by individuals or groups of individuals on a commercial basis.

The country has five national public universities with a student enrolment of 45,000 and four major private universities (together with other degree-awarding bodies applying for university status). There are three national polytechnics and twelve institutes of technology offering skills training in the rural areas.

Information provision

An overview of information systems in Kenya has been given by this writer in a previous article (Odini, 1993). It was observed that the country has a fairly good information infrastructure which forms a solid base on which information services can develop.

The importance of information services in general as a vital resource for national development is unquestionable. There is, however, a need for improved access to information by the various user groups and for the availability of information at the right time and in an appropriate form. Regrettably, the information systems in the country are under-utilized owing to various factors such as the prevalence of information services which have been designed without a proper analysis of the needs of users, high levels of illiteracy and language barriers. However, there is still ample opportunity for information experts in Kenya to stimulate the use of information if more attention is paid to the information needs of the various groups and the communication process among each group of the user community.

Although Kenya has no comprehensive information policy, there are several sectoral policies in the form of legislation, regulations and guidelines, covering, for instance, public libraries (Kenya National Library Service (KNLS) Board Act); archives (Public Archives Act); deposit material (Books and Newspapers Act); Sessional Paper No. 5 of 1982 dealing with science and technology information; and District Focus Circular No. 1/86 on the establishment of District Information and Documentation Centres. Other relevant laws include the Copyright Act, Universities Act, Education Act and Sessional Paper No. 6 of 1988.

Kenya's national information systems comprise the nation's libraries, documentation centres, archives, records centres and learning resource centres. These systems are supported and made effective by other agencies dealing with the generation, enumeration, and transfer of information such as the publishing industry, statistical bureaux, telecommunications, informatics and the mass media.

Although little documentation is available on the use of information by the school population in the country, it is believed that this group makes greater use of information services provided in the country than other groups of the user community, for example: farmers and rural communities; professionals in various fields; policy makers; and administrators. However, the prevailing teaching methods give little encouragement to the development of free personal enquiry. There is much dependence on 'chalk and talk' with little library usage, since students/pupils do not need to obtain ideas from various sources to pass examinations. This is unfortunate since it is in early life that a taste for books and the habit of using libraries and their resources or educational materials are most easily acquired (Aina, 1984).

There is little locally-published reading material for children in Kenya. Furthermore, there is no official policy requiring schools (neither primary and secondary) to have libraries. School libraries are not given any official support from the government. It is left to the initiative of heads of schools and Parents Associations to establish, equip and maintain libraries in their own schools.

Some headteachers use some of the funds meant for sports and other related extra-curricula activities to establish and stock their school libraries. Old schools, especially those in urban areas which were established during the colonial period, generally have better school libraries than relatively new ones in the rural areas. Schools with adequate school libraries include Starehe Boys Centre, Nairobi School, Pangani Girls, Lenana School, Alliance High School (both boys and girls) and Kenya High School. Resources in these libraries comprise both printed materials in the form of books and periodicals as well as non-book media such as audio-visual materials.

Although some school libraries therefore continue to be developed to support the education system, their development is not uniform throughout the country but tends to favour urban schools at the expense of rural ones. The majority of the school population are denied access to a reasonable variety of educational materials. In order to address this problem, the Ministry of Education incorporated Teachers Advisory Centres (TACs) in the Inspectorate Section in the early 1970s with an aim of enabling teachers in primary schools to access educational materials such as books and audio-visual equipment. It was hoped that the use of Teachers Advisory Centres by teachers would improve teaching standards through improved instruction and the loan of classroom materials.

A similar initiative took place at the secondary level, with 26 Learning Resource Centres (LRCs) being established during the early 1990s. These were part of a British Department for International Development (DFID) supported programme, the Secondary English Language Project (SELP). An element within the project was the provision of English language materials and the Resource Centres were set up to manage these. They aimed to provide materials for those teaching in secondary schools in the district surrounding the Centre. DFID supplied reference and text-books (not only for English language teaching but in all subjects of the secondary curriculum) and class sets of reading books to each Resource Centre, as well as typewriters, duplicating machines and stationery. The British NGO Voluntary Service Overseas (VSO) provided the first Learning Resource Centre managers. However the usefulness of the Centres has been limited by the fact that many schools are not members, either because they are unaware of its services or because they do not want to pay the annual subscription. The Learning Resource Centres have not become self-sustainable but still rely on donations. Moreover, many of the teachers who were trained through the SELP project, either locally or in the UK, have left secondary schools for better paying jobs in colleges or universities.

Teachers Advisory Centres

The Kenya government through the School Inspectorate of the Ministry of Education attaches great importance to continuing education programmes for teachers. Teacher education is conceived of as a career-long process in order to avoid situations such as those reported by the World Bank:

> ... many schools in developing countries fail to reach or teach children because available resources are not used efficiently and effectively by the teachers concerned ... . (World Bank, 1990)

Kahn (1991) reports that centres for teachers and resources have been established worldwide. These centres, despite their varying names (Learning Resource Centres, Pedagogical Centres and Advisory Centres), have the common characteristic of providing classroom support for teachers. Teachers must be trained not only to develop their pupils' reading ability but also to encourage independent learning and the acquisition of good information skills. Co-operation among the stakeholders and particularly between teachers and Teachers Advisory Centre Tutors (TAC tutors) is essential to there being an effective collection of resources to match pupils' and teachers' needs and in the provision of appropriate resources in general. A TAC tutor must be able to ascertain the information needs of the Centre's user group. Adequate financial support is essential for the success of the operations of a Teachers Advisory Centre. Unless the centres are well funded they cannot carry out their functions effectively and many good plans proposed will not be implemented.

Origins, history and development

The need for establishing Teachers Advisory Centres was identified and incorporated in the 1969 plan for the establishment of a primary school inspectorate. The first TACs came into existence in 1970, one in Siriba College (currently Maseno University College) and another in Kagumo College. The plan stipulated that each district should have one TAC but two were to be established in each of the larger districts. UNICEF agreed to provide some of the basic equipment including tools, books and audio-visual equipment. The Kenya government was to provide buildings, personnel and recurrent expenditure for the centres.

By the mid-1970s, TACs had been established all over the country and most districts had at least one centre as per the initial government plan. Since it was difficult for many teachers to get the centres due to vast travelling distances, several sub-centres, referred to as zonal centres, were established in each district. A sub-centre was situated among a cluster of schools in an area where teachers could easily get together for a meeting. The sub-centres were initially meant to serve merely as convenient meeting places but were later to be supplied with some basic equipment and educational materials. They had caretakers, appointed from among the teachers in the schools where they were situated, to look after them.

However, the TAC programme faced severe problems when UNICEF stopped financing it. It was not possible to stock and sustain the TACs as planned using the meagre national resources. The shortage of funds provided for the establishment and maintenance of TACs led to the following problems:

- many centres were housed in poor and badly equipped buildings which were originally meant to be store rooms in the District Education Officer's building block or classrooms which had been converted into centres. In addition to the problem of poor accommodation, many centres had no facilities for the making and display of teaching/learning resources, no library facilities and no facilities for home science;
- many centres lacked any form of transport to bring either the TAC tutor or resource materials to those teachers who were unable to visit the centres;
- most of the TAC tutors had not received any special training for the task they were expected to undertake. As a result of this each TAC tutor operated their centre in the way they thought best.

In 1978 the Permanent Secretary in the Ministry of Education established 'The Primary Teacher Updating Committee' to examine the possibility of developing and setting up a 'Primary Teacher Up-dating Programme'. This Committee examined the TAC programme in detail and recommended that:

- the role of TACs in advising and updating teachers and in carrying out research at the local level must be made clear to all TAC staff;
- the number of TACs must be increased to give an adequate

service to teachers and these centres must be established in central and accessible venues;
- staff must be increased to enable the TACs to fulfil their role effectively;
- TACs should be housed in appropriately designed and equipped buildings.

The Committee suggested that a TAC should have the following:
- facilities
  - lecture, display and home science rooms;
  - office and store;
  - workshop;
  - library;
  - sanitation unit;
- resources and equipment
  - curriculum material currently in use in primary schools, professional reference books including books on teaching methodology;
  - tools suitable for making teaching/learning resources;
  - audio-visual resources including: radio/cassette player, overhead projector, slide projector, camera;
  - reprographic equipment including: typewriters and duplicating machines;
  - a portable electricity generator;
  - home science equipment;
- a van for transport – the Committee noted that it was essential that TAC staff be able to travel with resource materials to teachers in the district;
- adequate finance for the effective running of the TACs. It was suggested that TACs be financed by the Inspectorate Headquarters and that funds be allocated to them through the DEO's Office.

Some of the recommendations made by the Committee, for example: outlining the role of TAC tutor; increasing the number of TACs; addition of more staff; have been implemented. However, due to lack funds, it has not been possible to implement many of the other recommendations.

TACs have benefited from the support provided by DFID from 1992 for the strengthening of primary education in Kenya. The first phase of this support aimed at raising the quality of teaching and learning in the core subject areas of mathematics, science and English by establishing TAC-based in-service training. As a part of this support, book boxes and resource materials, including a package of consumables, were distributed to 239 zonal TACs and 42 district TACs. DFID also assisted with the construction of 61

TACs. However, this support has not been uniformly distributed throughout the country. Those districts which are relatively disadvantaged in socio-economic development have received greater supplies of educational materials than others.

Functions

Teachers Advisory Centres were established to carry out the following functions:

- provide convenient and appropriately equipped centres for updating teachers;
- prepare and produce support materials for use on updating courses and in any follow-up activities required;
- carry out research in primary teaching methods and the use of locally available teaching resources and communicate the results of such researches to the classroom teachers and national curriculum specialists at the Kenya Institute of Education (KIE);
- take an active part in the development of the primary school curriculum by maintaining close and adequate contact with the teachers and local subject panels, so that relevant feedback may be readily available when research and assessment of various programmes are called for;
- provide educational counselling services not only for the teachers but for the community as a whole;
- act as a receiving centre for various resource materials from agencies like KIE and also act as distributing centres for these materials;
- by working closely with teachers colleges, help expose students to what goes on in primary schools and how to use TACs when they leave college.

Providing access to educational materials was thus one of their many functions.

Governance

The Teachers Advisory Centres, as a national service, are administered by the Ministry of Education's Inspectorate Section. In the field, TACs are run by centre tutors who report to their respective District Inspectors of Schools.

The tutors work in close collaboration with their respective area assistant primary school inspectors and principals of the primary teachers colleges where the centres are situated, since they are responsible for TAC operations and for providing the Ministry of Education with a record and evaluation of their work. KIE, a body responsible for curriculum research and development, works with the TACs in collaboration with the Inspectorate.

Target user population

The user population comprises teachers in primary schools within close proximity to a TAC, usually within a radius of ten kilometres. This is usual in small-sized and more developed districts which have a higher school population. However, in large districts with few schools spread out over great distances and with poor access roads, it is common to find TACs located very far away from their target user populations.

Methodology

Choice of methodology and rationale

A preliminary workshop was held in London in September 1997, see Chapter One, attended by local researchers. The case study approach, employing mainly semi-structured interviews, was chosen for the survey since it was particularly suitable for providing an in-depth analysis of accessibility to educational materials in Teachers Advisory Centres by the school population. The case study methodology enabled the researcher to concentrate on specific instances or situations and to identify the various interactive processes at work in TACs. Some of these processes might have remained hidden in a larger scale survey.

It was felt that the case study approach was the only approach that would be able to provide data which would determine efficiency, effectiveness and economy. However, care was taken to ensure that the country context within which the Teachers Advisory Centre operated was not ignored since the success or failure of the TACs could not be determined in isolation, without due regard to the contribution made by other similar modalities such as school libraries. The case study method therefore involved collecting relevant background information or data from schools, school inspectors, education officials, TAC tutors and teachers.

Data collection and analysis

Data was collected in general discussions that this researcher held with several teachers, TAC tutors and education officials on several occasions.

Documents about the country and Teachers Advisory Centres in particular were studied, including official government statistics. **122** With regard to TACs, data was obtained from annual reports and several unpublished records and articles written by education officials, school inspectors and TAC tutors.

The main research instrument, however, consisted of a semi-structured interview framework for obtaining information on user satisfaction and impact which was administered to teachers by this researcher assisted by postgraduate students at the Faculty of Information Sciences in Moi University. The main analytical approach employed in this study was based on a framework developed by Orr in 1993 and concentrated on outputs – value, effectiveness and benefits. In assessing performance, emphasis was placed on economy, efficiency, effectiveness and user satisfaction, market penetration and cost-effectiveness.

Sample

The study was conducted in Uasin Gishu district of Rift Valley Province. The district is divided into zones and a Teachers Advisory Centre had been established to serve primary school teachers in each zone. Six zones were selected for the study based on their geographical location and after consultation with the District Inspector of Schools. Three schools were selected in each of the six zones but an attempt was made to include one school which was in close proximity to the TAC, one which was located mid-way between the TAC and the zonal boundary and one which was furthest or among the furthest away from the TAC. Since there were six zones considered for the study, a total of 18 schools were selected.

Six teachers in each of the sampled schools were selected for interview employing a sampling technique to ensure that both TAC users and non-users were included in the sample. This was important since the researcher was interested in hearing from both groups. A total of 108 teachers were interviewed in the district.

Problems

During the preparations for this survey, teachers went on a nationwide strike demanding higher salaries. By the time the teachers resumed their normal duties, there were only two weeks left before an early vacation for most of the school population. The early vacation meant that the appointments and interviews with more than one hundred teachers had to be conducted within a period of only two weeks. To resolve this problem, permission was granted to involve postgraduate students of Information Sciences at Moi University in data collection.

However, since the time available for the case study data collection was so limited, even with the assistance of research assistants (students) it would still have been very difficult to extend the study to another district – a disadvantaged district – and to include the Learning Resource Centres set up to serve secondary school teachers, as earlier planned. A decision was therefore made to confine the study to Uasin Gishu district and to Teachers Advisory Centres serving primary schools.

One other problem encountered during the course of the study was the lack of statistical data for analytical purposes. TAC tutors hardly kept any records, for example the number of users over a given period of time, number of books borrowed, and so forth. In some cases this problem was overcome by taking statistics over a two week period and extrapolating the findings in order to obtain a reasonable estimate covering a longer period.

Findings

Collection development

Data analysis was conducted in order to assess the sufficiency and relevance of the available stock, to identify the selection/acquisition practices employed by the TACs, and to find out the ways in which the collections were organized. Both quantitative and qualitative means were employed to analyze the data.

Data analysis revealed that although one of the main functions of the Teachers Advisory Centres was to provide convenient and appropriately equipped centres for updating teachers and to act as receiving and distributing centres for various educational resource materials, not one of the TACs studied had sufficient relevant educational materials for the school population that it was meant to serve. Throughout the Uasin Gishu district where this study was conducted, TACs appear to be in a state of crisis and this researcher believes that TACs are actually in decline throughout the country. The school population cannot have their information needs fully met by the TACs or Learning Resource Centres.

A typical response given by the teachers in interviews in reply to the question about the sufficiency and relevance of educational materials in the TACs was 'The materials are not sufficient and are irrelevant to my needs ...'

Each TAC had an average of about 800 educational items only, including books, maps and wall charts. The only TAC which had a total stock of more than 1000 items had received aid in the form of book donations from DFID. The books comprised English story books, but these were obviously inadequate in view of the fact that the TAC was meant to serve about 500 teachers.

The subject coverage of the collections available left a lot to be desired. None of the TACs possessed a comprehensive stock to cover all the primary school curriculum subjects. Most of the

TACs had reasonably good collections of atlases and wall charts for geography, history and civics, but they all had inadequate stock in other subjects such as science, mathematics, art, craft and music.

Although local subject panels had been established at zonal level to assist TAC tutors in the selection and acquisition of educational materials as recommended by the Primary Teacher Updating Committee of 1978, the subject panels had become dormant in five out of the six zones in which this study was conducted. It was however, encouraging to note that in one zone where some subject panels were proactive, the teachers were involved in the preparation and selection of educational materials for their TAC.

Collection development was generally not well organized and, in actual fact, none of the TACs had a well formulated and regularly reviewed collection development policy that would guide the development of their stock. There was no attempt, for example, to review the existing state of affairs, review relative strengths and weaknesses, consider environmental influences and other current trends, set goals and design strategies to reach those goals.

Staffing

Although the Primary Teacher Updating Programme Committee recommended that staff of TACs be increased, this study found that the recommendation had not been implemented. Each TAC is run by only one tutor, who opens the TAC only two days a week on average and spends the rest of the days in the field visiting schools to meet and discuss teaching methods, curriculum and other educational matters with teachers. All the teachers who were interviewed underlined the need for TAC staffing to be increased so that the TAC could be open throughout the week. The practice of keeping the TACs closed during the time when the TAC tutor was away in the field was a major discouraging factor to teachers in visiting and accessing educational materials in the TACs. A typical statement which was recorded in several interviews with the teachers was as follows:

> ... The TAC is rarely open since the tutor is never around whenever I visit the TAC. I think he spends all his time in the field. I have ceased to use it.

It is the inadequate staffing leading to very irregular opening which has discouraged many teachers from visiting the resource centres. The problem of irregular opening hours was aggravated by a lack of records and publicity on what information resources are available; even those centres which have benefited from donor aid continue to be shunned by teachers, who still see TACs as unimportant channels for accessing educational materials.

125   TAC staffing needs to be increased and staff need to develop attributes that will make teachers see them as dependable providers of useful educational materials.

TAC tutors' qualifications range from Primary 2 to Secondary 1 grade, since the posts are localized and take into account environmental knowledge. For example, a teacher with Primary 2 certificate with a wealth of knowledge about Narok district in Maasailand may be selected as a TAC tutor in Narok rather than a Secondary 1 teacher with a higher academic qualification but little local knowledge of Narok district.

Teachers who are appointed as TAC tutors go through a rigorous assessment procedure. However, there is no additional training for TAC tutors, and many teachers felt that some TAC tutors were not performing their duties effectively, because they lacked the necessary training. This is probably true since TAC tutors did not, in particular, possess good skills in collecting, organizing educational materials and disseminating information to the school population that they were appointed to serve, the sort of skills normally acquired through training in library and information studies rather than in teacher training.

Moreover, the level of information consciousness – the value that the TAC tutors placed on information as a resource – was not high enough among the TAC tutors who were interviewed. This was best exemplified by their lukewarm support and encouragement for the exploitation by teachers of information resources from the collections in their TACs. The low level of information consciousness among the TAC tutors was manifested in a diversity of ways: the practice of keeping educational materials locked up in cabinets; the complete lack of information retrieval tools; the habit of keeping the TACs closed several days in a week; and the failure to make any attempt to assess the information needs of the school population that they were meant to serve. There was, however, some variation among individual TAC tutors with regard to the level of information consciousness.

Physical facilities

Physical facilities were generally poor in all the TACs. The limited educational materials were housed in small rooms, some of which also served as offices for zonal inspectors of schools. Some centres were originally classrooms which had been converted into Teachers Advisory Centres.

Since most teachers used the TACs very rarely, not many of them saw the poor physical facilities as a major problem. They did not seem to bother or complain about the few old and dusty reading tables and chairs commonly found in many TACs. Whenever the teachers visited TACs, they appeared to be preoccupied with identifying the needed items and had no time to think about the poor state of the physical facilities.

None of the TACs visited had proper shelving facilities. Books and other educational materials were kept in boxes or locked up in cabinets which were opened only when items were required by a user. The materials were not maintained in open access stacks, where they could be freely consulted.

Finance

Teachers Advisory Centres require both capital and recurrent expenditure but are dependent on such donations as are given. TACs, as providers of educational materials, are actually not sustainable at the moment. Their decline has been most acute over the last decade.

For the past ten years the Kenyan economy has been declining, inflation combined with recession has produced higher prices for educational materials in general and books in particular. This has caused severe problems for the country's educational resource centres, including libraries, which are squeezed from two directions: their sources of revenue have been drying up while costs of reading materials have continued to increase. Acquisition budgets have been particularly severely affected and most of the TACs do not get any funds from the government for the purchase of educational materials.

Several TAC tutors reported that they had not received any capital funding for the purchase of educational materials for the last five to six years. The only form of funding that they have received has been for their monthly salaries. The only TACs which have received reading materials in the recent past are those which have benefited from DFID donations.

Use

Data analysis revealed that 75% of the teachers interviewed had visited their zonal or district TAC at least once, but that 40% of this group had ceased to use them. Four major reasons were identified for visits to TACs by the teachers who participated in this study. These were:
- to attend seminars or workshops organized by the TAC tutor to receive updates in teaching methods;
- to represent their schools on zonal examination panels in their respective subjects especially for purposes of examination moderation;
- to participate in the preparation of teaching aids in their subject areas;
- to access educational materials in their respective subjects.

It was interesting to note that although the provision of access to educational materials to the school population was one of the main functions of TACs, only 20% of the teachers who were interviewed cited access to educational materials as the main reason for visiting TACs.

TACs gave out hardly any materials on loan to their user communities. The inadequate materials stocked were restricted to reference use.

This study found that, although the provision of access to education materials and information services were central to the mission of TACs, they had shifted away from this mission and were more involved in examination matters at the expense of information services. It was therefore not surprising to find that none of the TACs studied offered any education programme to their users in the use of informational materials in education.

Many respondents reported that since their zonal TAC had very little or nothing to offer in terms of supplementary reading material, they used the main public library in Eldoret to access a wide variety of reading materials. They saw the public library as the only source of educational materials not available in their own schools. Teachers in private schools reported that they turned to their school library for supplementary reading materials. These teachers hardly visited TACs since they were convinced that their own school library was far better stocked than TACs in terms of educational materials. Whereas teachers in government schools, most of which did not have school libraries, relied on the public library for educational materials, those in private schools relied on their own school libraries. It was clear that Teachers Advisory Centres were not important sources of supplementary educational materials to the school population.

Evaluation

Costs and cost-effectiveness

Good information should be cost effective, that is, the value of the information should be more than the cost of acquiring it. Cost is therefore an important consideration in the provision of information services. However, it is important to bear in mind that information services are not easily tangible or measurable and it is difficult to express them in monetary terms.

The structure of costs that are related to the provision of information products or services comprise the following elements:
- direct costs (materials equipment, consumables, salaries);
- indirect costs (overheads/training, management/supervision, building costs, central charges).

These costs may be:
- fixed costs (do not change with volume of use);
- variable costs (dependent on number of activities undertaken or vary according to usage).

If the above cost elements are known, it is possible to work out the total costs of an information service. It is regrettable that in this study it was not possible to work out meaningful direct and indirect costs, since most of the Teachers Advisory Centres studied had not received any information resources in the last six years. Most actually were dormant and stocked with a few old and outdated books acquired a decade or so ago. It was difficult in this survey to conduct any useful costing of the services of the TACs in their current state since apart from staff salaries the other cost elements could not be ascertained. That said, the costs of providing reading materials would be low, as only part of the time of the TAC tutor was utilized, the premises were not pupose built but were existing buildings, and materials were received on donation rather than purchased.

Yet, however low the costs, cost-effectiveness was even lower. As revealed in this study, teachers who used Teachers Advisory Centres were dissatisfied with the services offered by the centres, especially with regard to the provision of educational materials. This dissatisfaction was revealed on a wide scale in the data collected in all the teacher interviews. The existing collections of educational materials in the centres are generally inappropriate and incapable of meeting the needs of teachers not only because they are inadequate and dated, but are also because their distance from many schools and their frequent closures make them difficult to access.

Effectiveness

This study has established that, despite all the good intentions of the Kenya government when they established Teachers Advisory Centres, the Centres have turned out to be completely ineffective in providing access to current and useful educational materials for the school population. The only supplementary reading materials that have been acquired have come as donations mainly from DFID, but these are barely adequate. Other materials commonly found in TACs include a few charts, maps and syllabuses which are already stocked by most schools.

TACs have suffered several years of neglect and have been in steady decline over the last decade to the extent that they have become marginalized. Moreover, it was clear from the data collected in the study that long distances coupled with poor public transport facilities discouraged many teachers from visiting the centres. Schools do not have their own buses and neither do they have funds to transport teachers to the resource centres. Furthermore, those teachers who used their own means of transport to get to the resource centres, were on many occasions disappointed to find the TACs either closed, or open but without the needed educational materials.

Impact

Dissatisfaction with the services of the resource centres, essentially stemming from a combination of poorly managed services, long distances from their work stations (schools), poor public transport system and a lack of suitable supplementary educational materials, made all teachers who were interviewed in this study report that the TACs had made very little or no impact on the education process among their pupils. None of the teachers believed that the establishment of a TAC in their zone had had any bearing on examination pass rates, drop-out and repetition rates or improved pupil learning, as evidenced by better reading skills or better critical abilities. Some of the teachers asserted that it would make no difference to their pupils' educational progress if their local TAC was closed down since it was serving no useful purpose especially with regard to the provision of educational materials.

Conclusion

Teachers Advisory Centres, as resource centres, were meant to provide accessibility to educational materials; but this role has been neglected in Kenya. It is most unfortunate that the importance of the centres as sources of a wide variety of reading materials has been overlooked for some time and, regrettably, there are no signs of any change to the current state of affairs at the moment or in the near future. The centres have therefore been of little benefit to the school population and have been ineffective in serving them.

Such centres have been ineffective in pursuance of their main functions in accordance with their mission and have resorted to performing peripheral functions such as coordinating zonal examinations.

Future of TACs

An evaluation of the numerous physical, psychological and other barriers to the use of Teachers Advisory Centres that have prevented them from providing effective information services to the school population shows that many of the constraints cannot be easily alleviated or avoided. There is a need, for example, to develop the transport and communications and the information infrastructure for improved access to information and for the availability of information at the right time and in an appropriate form. It is also clear from the findings of this study that Learning Resource Centre staff, commonly referred to as TAC tutors, require extensive training in communication and interpersonal skills, collection development, organization of resources and information dissemination in order to play an effective role in serving the school population. TAC tutors need to set standards of performance for themselves and to create an atmosphere of cordiality to motivate teachers to use their centres. Good human relations between TAC tutors and teachers is a prerequisite for good user/staff relations.

Another important consideration for TAC tutors must be the evaluation of their collections and services and their relevance to the needs of the school population. This implies that needs must first be known and understood before they can be met. However, many past studies have recognized the fact that ascertaining information needs is not a simple matter. To be able to design appropriate information systems for the school population, TAC staff need to conduct qualitative user studies research aimed at gathering information on the knowledge and skills required to improve the communication process among the various members of the school population.

For TACs to provide a more effective service, staff must be prepared at all times to offer user-centred and user-friendly service to the school population. They should be concerned with 'customer care' and should give adequate publicity to the facilities and services offered by the centre, since resources and services which are not known will not be used. TAC tutors should use modern marketing strategies in putting their message across to the school population.

In view of the prevailing economic hardships in the country it is highly unlikely that the above measures will be taken now or in the near future to salvage the deterioration of the provision of information resources by TACs to the school population. Future prospects offer little comfort; indeed, present projections suggest that the part played by TACs in providing educational materials to the school population in the country will be further undermined.

Future strategies on school level information provision

This study was conducted in one district but the picture is more or less the same all over the country. It is clear that Teachers Resource Centres or Learning Resource Centres have not proved to be either cost-effective or effective in providing educational materials to the school population in Kenya.

There is, therefore, a need to devise new strategies on school level information provision. This author believes that providing teachers with relevant resources in their own school libraries will make the resources more accessible so that they are used more, will improve lesson presentation and contribute to a better pass rate of pupils. Moreover, school library resources accessed and used by pupils themselves will promote independent learning and inculcate a reading habit in the pupils. Pupils will be enabled to gain knowledge of the sources of information and develop the skills needed to retrieve and use information. Teachers Advisory Centres should continue to play the role of arranging and offering in-service training to teachers especially in modern teaching methods but should leave information provision role to a more effective modality.

Chapter Eight

VILLAGE READING ROOMS: BOTSWANA
ANNE HEWLING

Background

Socio-economic and political context

Botswana is a land-locked country in the centre of the Southern African Plateau. Most of the population lives in the eastern region, which straddles the north-south railway line. The rest of Botswana is covered with the Kalahari desert which accounts for around two-thirds of the land area of the country. The whole country suffers from lack of water. Drought has been persistent since the early 1980s (Botswana, 1997:3).

At Independence in 1966, Botswana was one of the poorest countries with a GDP of around US$8.2 million with *per capita* income at US$80. By 1996 GDP had risen to US$4.6 billion with *per capita* income at US$3,100 (Botswana, Ministry of Finance and Development Planning, 1991) mainly due to the discovery of large diamond deposits around the time of Independence.

Most of the population comes from Setswana-speaking ethnic groups. The official languages are Setswana and English, the latter being the main language of government and education. The most recent census, in 1991, yielded a *de facto* population of 1,326,796 compared with 574,094 in 1971 and 941,027 for 1981. About 15% of the 1991 population were under 5 years old and about 43% were younger than 15 years. The population is small relative to the size of the country, but it is growing rapidly as a result of high fertility and declining mortality rates.

Educational policies and practices

In the thirty years since Botswana became an independent nation (having previously been a British Protectorate) school enrolment at primary level has improved steadily to over 90% and most primary school leavers are able to find places in Form One of the secondary system. Places are available for all children, a priority is to improve drop-out rates. School attendance is not compulsory at present although this remains a long term aim.

Policy for educational development and standards is embodied in the Revised National Policy on Education (RNPE) of 1994 which was the outcome of the presidential commission of enquiry set up in 1992. The RNPE reintroduced the 7-3-2 system: seven years are spent in primary school, three in junior secondary and two in senior secondary. The first ten years of schooling form the period of basic education to which all children have a right. At the end of ten years, Junior Certificate examinations are held after which there are two options: an academic route through senior secondary school and Cambridge 'O' level exams or a vocational route through apprenticeship or other vocational training course. Admission to university is possible according to performance on completion of either route. The current National Development Plan (NDP 8, Botswana, 1997) has a target figure of 50% for the number of children progressing from the basic education programme to the academic route through senior secondary school.

The medium of instruction is Setswana in Standards 1 to 4 and thereafter English, although it is intended that from the year 2003 English will become the medium of instruction from Standard 2.

The 1993 Literacy Survey showed an illiteracy rate of 31%. The Botswana Government has placed great importance on improving literacy and a well-developed National Literacy Programme was founded in 1981 with the aim of eradicating illiteracy by 1985. This turned out to be unrealistic and the plan was given a longer life through NDP 6 and continues still. Between 1981 and 1991, according to data from the Department of Non-Formal Education (DNFE), the numbers of participants in national literacy programmes varied between 19 and 35 thousand at any one time. Unfortunately the data does not show success and failure rates so it is difficult to interpret why numbers in the programme vary so greatly. The Revised National Policy on Education (Botswana, 1994) states that in terms of numbers the programme has been the largest in any area of out-of-school education:

> ... but its focus has been on teaching basic literacy so that the post-literacy phase has been relatively neglected ... a number of initiatives have been taken ... including the establishment of village reading rooms in conjunction with the Botswana National Library Service [and] the publication of some booklets for new literates....
> (Botswana, 1994:279)

NDP 7 and NDP 8 also place emphasis on this area and the expansion of basic literacy to include an Adult Basic Education Course equivalent to Standard 7 (the final year of primary school) (Botswana, 1994:353). Other literacy-related aims in NDP 8 are 'to sustain a literate environment through the provision of post-literacy reading materials' and 'to strengthen the inter-agency materials production and publication of stories for neo-literates and people with low reading abilities' (Botswana, 1994:373).

The total budget for education for the year 1999–2000 is in the region of US$480 million of which US$300 million is for recurrent expenditure, including US$44 million for the University of Botswana. US$122 million will be spent on development expenses for plans laid down by the Revised National Policy on Education (RNPE) (*Daily News* 11/03/99). The annual unit cost for educating a student at primary level will be US$270 per child and at secondary level US$890 per child, excluding development costs for the RNPE (*Daily News* 23/04/99). The budget is huge and reflects the importance placed on education by the government. The RNPE has a lifespan of 25 years and is a cornerstone of government policy. NDP 8 makes it very clear:

> A productive and highly motivated workforce is fundamental to achieving *Sustainable Economic Diversification* [the theme of NDP 8]. During NDP 8, the education sector will contribute to producing such a workforce through continued implementation of the recommendations of the Revised National Policy on Education of 1994. ... In particular, emphasis will be on quality at all levels, cost recovery and effectiveness, vocational education and gender neutrality. (Botswana, 1997:337)

In 1996 the total primary school population was 319,136 in 759 schools, with an average of 440 per school. The prediction for 2000 is a primary school population of 338,720.

Information provision

Radio Botswana operates two channels one of which is extensively used to broadcast educational and schools programmes and material. There is currently no national television station but this is being established and should be on air by the end of 2000. There are four 'national' newspapers which publish on a weekly basis but have circulations which seldom exceed 20,000. The only daily newspaper is the *Daily News*, a government paper which is distributed free of charge.

The Botswana National Library Service (BNLS) was set up in 1966 by Act of Parliament to promote literacy, facilitate access to educational materials and enhance the intellectual development of the nation by providing library services countrywide (Botswana, 1997:436). Kotei, in a 1984 study towards developing a national book policy for Botswana, comments that:

> ... the Act stipulates 'comprehensive and efficient library services for all persons desiring to make use hereof'. This particular requirement has been observed more in promise than in practice. The sheer

geographical size ... puts many isolated settlements out of reach ... a book stock of 200,000 cannot be shared equitably among a population approaching one million .... (Kotei and Milazi, 1984:61)

In fact the Botswana Library Service *has* provided library access for very wide numbers of people in a short period of time. In addition to large library facilities in Gaborone and Francistown, the Library Service has seventeen branch libraries around the country as well as facilities in three major community colleges (junior secondary schools) and a huge network of outreach services ranging from the Village Reading Rooms (VRRs), of which there are currently 64 operating countrywide, to a book box service and books by post. Village Reading Rooms are described by the Library Service as:

Small libraries in rural areas where the book box service does not operate. They are housed in either primary school classrooms or buildings provided by Village Development Committees. They cater for new literates, schools and the general public. (BNLS, 1998)

The formulation of a National Book Policy was first suggested in the 1970s but has yet to materialize in any fully fledged form. Difficulties have lain in establishing exactly what should be included and where responsibility for it should lie. Kotei's 1984 study addresses many of the issues and comes up with positive suggestions, but responsibility for follow-up on these has been divided between different bodies and as a result many have gone unattended to. Currently both the Ministry of Labour and Home Affairs and the Ministry of Education are looking at related issues. One initiative that Kotei praised, the development of Village Reading Rooms, has been adopted and expanded and may be said to give the widest geographical access so far to reading materials for the general public – although this was not their initial target population.

At the time of Kotei's study, books and library provision for schools was still limited. Only 30 out of 47 government secondary schools and colleges had libraries and only 33 out of 455 primary schools had any kind of book provision via the book box service. Currently all junior and senior secondary schools and colleges have library facilities although not all are fully stocked or staffed. The book box service covers primary schools without access to other library facilities.

Responsibility for library provision in schools is however a vexed issue since, as a result of historical precedence, it has been split between the Library Service and the Ministry of Education. The Library Service retains responsibility for provision of librarians in senior secondary schools while the Ministry of Education is responsible for training those in junior secondary schools. The

136 Library Service retains responsibility for overall professional development in all government ministries. Since the Library Service does not have adequate trained staff to send to senior secondary schools and the Ministry of Education does not have enough teachers to release to be trained as librarians for junior secondary schools, provision of an adequate service still cannot be assured.

The Revised National Policy on Education recommended that a separate school library service be set up but this seems unlikely to occur in the short term (Botswana, 1993:186). However, provision is made in NDP 8 for construction of libraries in some larger primary schools (NDP 8: project LG1102) and continued expansion of the village reading room service at the rate of thee new villages per year. Branch libraries are also set for expansion under NDP 8 (NDP 8: project HA514).

In the context of a National Book Policy, the Revised National Policy on Education also endorses endeavours to improve local book production capacity. The full recommendation reads:

> It is recommended that as a support to the development of education and the promotion of literacy, a National Book Policy be developed by the Ministry of Labour and Home Affairs to:
> a) promote local book production and ensure a high standard of professionalism in the book industry; and
> b) promote a culture of reading amongst Batswana. (Botswana, 1993:187)

Increasing numbers of books are being published in Botswana but constraints against expansion exist on several levels. Not the least of these is a lack of local capacity for quality printing, particularly colour printing. Anything but the most basic work must still be sent to South Africa or elsewhere for production. Faced with the choice of stocking attractively coloured, glossy materials from outside Botswana, usually in English, and the option of much poorer quality, though equally worthy, local material, it is not hard to see why local bookshops support so little local publishing. This has had a considerable knock-on effect on the materials to be found in libraries countrywide.

The Village Reading Rooms

History

The Village Reading Room (VRR) service was initiated in 1986 as a pilot exercise in twenty villages in the Kgatleng district. The first evaluation was extremely positive and the project was extended countrywide so that by 1994, when the second evaluation took place, there were no less than 54 in operation. The programme continues to this day although the rate of expansion has dropped from ten to three new sites per year. The reading rooms were designed to support and extend library services to literacy graduates. Mutanyatta and Mchombu state: 'as envisaged in the original blueprint, the role of the VRR was to provide post-literacy materials for the maintenance of literacy skills. Also to promote reading habits amongst rural inhabitants' (1995:114). They were to be a joint project by adult educators from the Department of Non-Formal Education (DFNE), Village Development Committees and the Library Service. The latter would provide specialist supervision and stock and the Village Development Committees would identify locations, usually primary school classrooms, provide staff, who would be DNFE adult educators, and pay honoraria. Staffing was on a volunteer basis since it would be provided by adult educators already in receipt of salaries from elsewhere. As time passed, problems arose over exact lines of command and staffing is now provided by the Library Service directly. Village Development Committees retain responsibility for premises and local services.

Although Village Reading Rooms were originally located in primary schools, and this remains the case for some locations, increasing numbers have been provided with free-standing, independent structures. These still rely heavily on primary school support and equipment, e.g. chairs and tables. Some structures now have electricity (via solar panels) which extends opening hours and access for users in employment who are unable to use the reading room during working hours. Most have a series of lockable metal cabinets fitted with shelves which house the library stock. Stock is purchased and supplied by an office in the Library Service Headquarters via the nearest branch library. Most is centrally selected although, increasingly, staff on the ground are being asked to identify areas of need. Generally speaking a reading room will be located in a village with a single primary school. In villages where there are two, the school not linked to the reading room will continue to receive a book box service. Kgatleng District has three such services, each with a collection of around 1000 to 1200 volumes.

Previous evaluations

The Village Reading Rooms have been much evaluated. The original pilot project was reviewed in 1986 when four of the twenty reading room were visited and investigated (Mchombu and Mutanyatta, 1987). The study concluded that the pilot project was highly successful and merited expansion. At that time, 71% of reading room users were primary school students looking for materials for study. 82% of respondents felt the stock adequately met their needs. Post-literacy students seem to have been using the reading rooms but not in the numbers envisaged originally. Lack of suitable collection materials at their level was one reason; most were adults faced with stocks of material for much younger readers.

The second major evaluation took place in 1995, with the same team of researchers. A summary of their findings is as follows:

- the main impact of the reading rooms has not been on the intended target group but on primary school children and their teachers;
- the primary school location, which permitted a low-cost approach and rapid expansion, has proved unpopular with the community;
- the materials in the reading rooms have successfully met the needs of the primary school children but not the needs of most adults in the community;
- the 'barefoot librarian' concept, which was adequate for a service with limited goals i.e. supplying materials to the newly literates, with low involvement of the Library Service and even lower involvement of DNFE, is unlikely to cope with demands for new services which go beyond services expected from a second generation of rural libraries – of which reading rooms are a classic example (Mutanyatta and Mchombu, 1995:109).

Functions

Village Reading Rooms are, in many ways, merely reduced sized libraries. They offer a range of materials and basic information services enabling users to borrow books and do basic research from a limited number of reference works. They also provide a study area for between ten and 25 users at any one time. Materials are available in English and Setswana, though the latter are very restricted in number, not so much because of any unequal purchasing policy but more as a reflection of the limited number of publications in that language in the market place generally.

Governance

Staff are recruited, trained and supervised by the Library Service. The entry qualification for staff is completion of primary school studies (Standard 7). Increasingly, the Library Service tries to recruit staff who have at least completed junior secondary studies, even if unsuccessfully, since the needs of users are becoming more complex. The grading of posts is fixed by the Department of Public Service Management; this places restrictions on the level of salaries that can be offered and thus limits the range of candidates who might otherwise present themselves for Village Reading Room posts. Post-holders are supervised, at intervals, by the Branch Librarian under whose jurisdiction the reading room lies, (usually the frequency of visits depends on the availability, or not, of government transport). Confusion among staff remains however, over day to day reporting lines and responsibilities. According to Mutanyatta and Mchombu:

> At the operational level, VRR assistants mentioned various people as their supervisors, 68% thought it was head teachers, while 16% thought it was literacy assistants, and another 16% thought it was the Village Development Committee Chairperson. Most said they had no written manual to guide them in their work (53%) but 37 % said they had some guidelines ... Such lack of clarity may lead to conflict when there is more than one supervisor, a fact which may confuse VRR assistants in terms of accountability. (1995:105 and vii)

Collection materials are provided by the Library Service who have a unit in their headquarters devoted to materials selection for the reading room network. The position of selecting materials is considered a 'stepping stone' to higher levels in the library service and thus staff turnover there is high. Many post-holders move on to promotion elsewhere after as little as twelve months. This means there are few personnel within the Library Service head-quarters who know what is suitable stock for a reading room.

The Library Service also supplies a range of Setswana materials especially commissioned for Village Reading Room post-literacy users. The current range covers 42 titles with further (unspecified) numbers planned under the NDP 8 project HA514.

The Village Development Committees are responsible for day to day non-professional matters in the VRR, the upkeep of buildings, etc. Where reading rooms are located in independent structures away from primary schools, these have usually been provided by the Development Committee.

Target user population

The Village Reading Rooms were intended to cater for post-literacy users to help them maintain their literacy skills. In fact, it is mainly primary school students who have benefited from their existence. There are several reasons for this:

- most reading rooms are located in or next to primary schools whereas post-literacy users are mainly adults who may not find it acceptable to use a facility situated in a primary school;

- most of the materials in reading rooms were originally

written with children in mind and although linguistically within the reach of post-literates they lack the tone and depth required by adult users;

- most materials are written in English which is suitable for school users but not for new literates who have only just achieved literacy in Setswana;
- although many reading rooms now have electricity that enables opening hours to include evenings, this is by no means the case everywhere. Coupled with the fact that many are not open at weekends, they become a non-resource for would-be adult users who are in employment during opening hours. This also inhibits use that may perpetuate and encourage a reading culture, which was the secondary aim of the Village Reading Rooms when they were established.

Mutanyatta and Mchombu noted that there was a need for better marketing of Village Reading Rooms services to all sectors of the community not just post-literacy students:

> A strategy is called for to motivate new literates from the DNFE National Literacy Programmes to meaningfully participate in the use of VRRs. Thus, there is need to step up marketing of the VRR to all villagers. Most of the VRR assistants mentioned that they were not conversant with promotion and publicity techniques. (1995:vi)

Interestingly all studies of Village Reading Rooms have shown an almost equal gender balance in their use.

The present case study

Methodology

The Village Reading Rooms have been closely and frequently evaluated. The present study saw no need to repeat past endeavours. Instead, it sought to re-evaluate much of the existing data from a new perspective – using the reading room network as a means of providing rural primary school students and their teachers with supplementary reading materials. From there it would be possible to assess whether this was a modality which could be used in other countries seeking to improve school students' access to books and information. In order to do this, discussions were held with the Library Service headquarters and branch library staff. Additional evaluation was done on a small scale through interviews with staff (four) and users (23) in four well-established reading rooms at Oodi, Rasesa, Matebele and Bokaa.

Three of the locations now had reading rooms based in independent structures although they had originally been based in primary schools. All structures are, however, close to the schools in which they were originally based. The reading room in Bokaa is still in the primary school. This proportion of independent to school-based reading rooms is thus roughly representative of the national pattern. In each case the reading room was the only type of library facility available to school students in the village.

The locations were chosen from the Kgatleng District where the original pilot project took place. This enabled an examination of longer standing, better established reading rooms since it was felt that this experience would provide a clearer indication of issues that might need to be addressed if the modality was to be used elsewhere. One staff member interviewed had been in post since the scheme's inception and was able to provide a perspective on fourteen years evolution of the concept of a Village Reading Room.

The four locations were between four and fifteen kilometres of a branch library. Staff reported that because of lack of local transport services it was unlikely that villagers, particularly school students, would use the branch library in preference to the Village Reading Room.

Questionnaires (copies are included in the Appendix) concentrated on the use of the reading room from the point of view of the primary school student, but were carefully designed to include many concepts and questions used in previous evaluations so that comparisons could be made of equivalent data.

Data was collected as objectively as possible but subjective assessment was made of such items as location, collection attractiveness, etc. where this was felt to have a bearing on the possible adaptation of the modality outside of Botswana.

Interviewee selection

Staff interviewed selected themselves by default. Users were selected at random within the guidelines that they must be equally divided male and female and all must be primary school students, whatever their ages. In fact, there was a preponderance of upper primary pupils, undoubtedly since their information needs are greater than those in the first few years of school life.

Problems

In order to be certain that questions and answers were fully understood, interviews took place in Setswana and responses were translated and recorded by the interviewer in English. This did not raise any problems but did mean that interviews took longer than anticipated because of slower recording of data.

142

Analysis and evaluation of findings

Collection size and development

All four reading rooms had originally opened in 1986 – and had thus featured in both of the evaluations carried out by Mchombu and Mutanyatta. Branch library records showed that over the period since inception they had received between 2,232 and 2,390 volumes each. No recent stock level data was readily available but it was estimated that current stock holdings are around 1,800 in each place. The difference is explained by books becoming damaged, worn out or lost. Examination of the overdue/lost books records showed that this is a major problem. The balance between children's and adult books is not recorded as such in library records but was estimated to be in the region of 60/40 children's to adults' books.

A guide to the cost of stock in any collection was given in the acquisitions registers in the branch library for the period 1994–1999. A rough average for children's books in 1994 was equivalent to US$4. By 1996 this was US$8 and in 1998 it was around US$10.

Comments on the adequacy of the materials were almost identical in each of the four locations. Existing materials, in terms of quantity and quality, were seen as useful and effective for primary school work. However, books were lacking in areas such as computers where materials date quickly and the base level data is so vast as to provide a serious problem for anyone wishing to cover the subject even at a basic level.

A universal lack of materials in Setswana was also noted. This comment reflects a real dilemma for any Library Service acquisitions librarian trying to cater for what, in this context, is a minority language. Faced with a severe shortage of any materials in that language, be they suitable for the readership or not, should quality or quantity prevail? And, with a limited budget, there is also the dilemma of whether to choose glossy, attractive books in English or less attractively presented works in Setswana. Several school students commented on how much they liked the colourful pictures and illustrations in some of the books; one reported his grades in art had improved as a result of exposure to such materials.

Although not commented on by interviewees, one researcher noted that many of the modern novels in one location were provided in large print format only, presumably in an attempt to make them more apparently accessible to the post-literate level of readership. Close study of the issues slips inside the books showed, however, little evidence of repeated use by anyone. More fiction and story books have been requested by almost all interviewees in all the evaluations. This investigation was no exception. Preference was indicated for *Pacesetters* and other Africa-based stories.

Staffing

All the staff interviewed had been given basic on the job training for the posts they occupied. All felt it was increasingly inadequate and lacking in depth, for example, not enough training had been given on how to do in-depth research on a given topic, given the needs of the current users of the facility and developments in information resources available globally. Their concerns were reflected by Mutanyatta and Mchombu:

> In their formative stage VRRs had a limited range of services which could easily be handled by a Standard 7 leaver. This strategy was attractive because payments would also be small. The findings of this study show that this innovation stage has now passed, and users are demanding a more mature service. (1995:111)

Physical facilities

Staff and users alike felt that physical provision of chairs, tables, etc. were inadequate for the demands of users, for example, the four locations ranged in capacity from eight to 23 seats. One staff member commented that she had been able to borrow chairs from the neighbouring primary school but now they wanted them back.

Regarding storage for books, this research raised no requests for more shelving, although Mutanyatta and Mchombu found in 1995 that some reading rooms had as much stock stored in cardboard boxes, inaccessible to readers, as could be displayed on shelves. Shelving in this context refers to space on shelves within lockable metal cupboards, not open shelves. The cupboards are a very effective way of securing the collections from the elements and from loss.

Use

Membership statistics for the four reading rooms for the survey month are shown in Table 8.1 overleaf.

Membership of the reading rooms is open to all, the books can be borrowed and taken away and read elsewhere. Table 8.2 gives the number of books borrowed in the survey month.

The reading rooms are mainly used by individuals, adults and children, though there is some class use too of those located in schools. Staff report that, when reading rooms relocated to independent structures, class use continued for some time but eventu-

Table 8.1 Village Reading Room membership statistics

Location (Population¹)	No. of members under 21 years	No. of adult members	Total membership
Oodi (2551)	109	126	235
Matabele (888)	115	154	269
Bokaa (3405)	131	125	256
Rasesa (2183)	158	104	262

¹ Population figures are from the 1991 national census

Table 8.2 Number of books borrowed from Village Reading Rooms in the survey month

Location	Fiction borrowed (by children)	Setswana books borrowed (by children)	Total books borrowed
Oodi	125	89	232
Matabele	27 (5)	11	45
Bokaa	9	4	29
Rasesa	59 (23)	37 (20)	156

ally dropped off. Since primary schools served by reading rooms have no other library facilities, this suggests that relocation may actually reduce many students use of and familiarity with library facilities and supplementary reading materials.

According to staff, use of the reading room for homework and school-related study was between 20% and 50%. Two of the four locations reported heavy usage by primary school staff for lesson preparation. Users reported attending with varying frequencies – daily in the case of one student who had nowhere at home to study. Two to three times a week was average and monthly or when school project work demanded, was another response from several users.

The older users, from Standard 6 and 7, suggested that separate areas for younger and older users would improve their ability to use the reading room since 'the young ones make too much noise'. This suggestion was endorsed by one of the staff interviewees too.

Effectiveness

Mutanyatta and Mchombu (1995) found that the users' principal perceived benefits from using the reading rooms were [an] 'improvement in English' (33%) and 'gained new ideas and knowledge' (22%). In these latest interviews, improvement in English was also noted as important as was gaining explanations for knowledge transmitted but not understood at school. Two respondents felt their grades had improved in school as a direct consequence of use of the reading room and nine out of twenty-three interviewees said they could read or write more fluently in English as a result of using the reading room. The longest serving member of staff noted that she had seen a definite improvement in school-leaving examination results in students who regularly used the facility.

Costs

Providing libraries in all primary schools and in all villages around Botswana would be prohibitively expensive. The reading room network extends the possibility of access to library facilities to a wide population in Botswana at a much lower cost. It is able to do this because:

- the same physical structure and staff are shared by the whole community;
- existing physical structures (primary schools) are used, or independent structures provided from community resources;
- infrastructure is simple and available locally, e.g. chairs, tables. Lockable cabinets replace traditional shelving;
- utility overheads are not high. Where electricity is available this comes from low-cost solar panels;
- staffing costs are low as staff are not qualified librarians and they live locally;
- management is on an occasional basis;
- stock is supplied centrally by the Library Service thereby ensuring maximum discounts.

The costs, either estimated or actual, of running the network of reading room were not available.

Overall assessment

There is no doubt that the Village Reading Rooms are providing a very necessary, useful and cost effective means of giving access to educational materials to school students in areas where no traditional library services operate. They are also offering the chance of library facilities to others in the community if they choose to use them. The range of materials is less suited to adult users but provides a gateway to other resources elsewhere in branch and national libraries. The nature of staffing and joint management by national and local bodies ensures that costs are kept as low as possible while providing what would otherwise be financially inaccessible resources for the grassroots population. Continued commitment by central government to literacy, culture and education ensures that such services will be expanded to other communities over coming years.

Conclusions

Attractive as Village Reading Rooms are, there remain a number of thorny issues to be considered before they are adopted as a model outside Botswana.

Finance

The costs for setting up a Village Reading Room network are huge. No direct analysis for Botswana has been done since the network has developed in a somewhat amorphous way. What is, however, clear is that it includes millions of US$ from the budgets of several different government departments. Costs to any one source could be reduced by sharing but this would involve:
- close, long term collaboration by several departments (and continued commitment to this);
- possible conflict of interest in the use of scare resources;
- possible conflict in lines of responsibility and thus possible inertia.

Staffing

Village Reading Room staff are central government employees with relatively low level qualifications recruited from the communities in which they work – since they were recruited on the basis of supporting post-literacy users needs only. All report that they feel inadequately trained for the demands of current Village Reading Room users. If reading rooms were to be set up from scratch today, in Botswana or elsewhere, it is unlikely that they could be staffed by those without formal librarianship or information provision qualifications. If qualified librarians needed to be employed a number of related issues would need to be addressed. Firstly they would require higher salaries. Secondly, given the often remote locations in which they would be working they would require incentives and support. Thirdly they would need to be part of a librarian cadre of some kind to enable this remote service to be part of a career structure.

Infrastructure

Botswana has relatively good internal communications: a wide network of tarred roads which increases annually and regular national bus and air services. The Central Transport Organisation which provides government vehicles is stretched but nevertheless does exist and provides a guarantee of transport albeit inadequate. Without this, the Library Service could not service the reading room network. Fuel is widely available. Many of these resources would not be available elsewhere on the continent and this would limit the effectiveness of any Village Reading Room programme.

The ever-expanding primary school building programme in Botswana ensures the existence of buildings in which to house reading rooms, even if preference would be for free standing structures. Such infrastructure might not be available elsewhere. Availability also relies on continuing good relations between different government ministries.

Botswana's Village Reading Rooms have shown, however, that lack of electricity need not be a problem through the use of solar panels designed for them by the Botswana Technology Centre.

Collection development

Village Reading Rooms in Botswana benefit, in cost effectiveness terms, from central provision of stock and materials enabling economies of scale simply because there are now so many of them. If stock were to be purchased for smaller numbers of facilities, or needed to be provided in minority languages, costs would be much higher and collections smaller and less useful or attractive to potential users. Any attempt to cater for a wider readership with an aim of increasing cost effectiveness would also diminish the power of the collection in terms of satisfying the needs of schools users.

Ethos and political will

Village Reading Rooms are an accidental success story in the context of providing access to educational materials for school students. They were established for the use of post-literacy, non-school attending students. Financial resources to start the programme were provided because of a will to assist literacy, not education. One must question whether such an investment would have received support if the aim from the outset were to provide libraries for primary students. Faced with the choice between libraries at this level and those at higher levels e.g. in secondary schools, one must question too whether investment at the lower level would be regarded as important enough. Experience in countries less well funded for education shows that libraries, even at secondary level, do not easily attract such funding as would be required to set up a Village Reading Room project from scratch. Similar comments might also be made around community funding for such a venture. Regrettably, most communities would have to rate primary level library services as a lower priority than most other developmental needs. The Village Reading Rooms of Botswana did receive a small amount of donor funding in the initial stages of development. Would donor funding be an option for any attempt to set up a similar programme elsewhere? Many funding agencies now require that their funds be spent on projects accorded high importance by the recipient government, which once again revives the question of political will in the face of a multiplicity of pressing needs. The total costs involved mean that NGO participation would be highly unlikely except in the short term provision of staffing/volunteer assistance.

Chapter Nine

CONCLUSIONS: ISSUES, OPTIONS AND STRATEGIES
DIANA ROSENBERG

Issues

The case studies highlight various issues which contribute to the effectiveness (or otherwise) of ways of providing access to supplementary reading materials by the school population in Africa.

Teacher involvement/training

Of primary importance, whatever the access/delivery model, is that teachers themselves have had some sort of training in teaching with books and are heavily committed to the need for the provision of supplementary reading materials. Too often in Africa the professional training of teachers has not stressed the importance of reading or equipped them to involve pupils in the learning process. The prevailing scholastic method depends on 'chalk and talk' and gives little encouragement to the development of free personal enquiry. The role of the teacher in a book-based approach cannot be over-estimated. Ideally they should be actively involved in the selection of materials. They must put aside time for silent reading, group reading, storytelling, voluntary reading. Unless teachers themselves are used to having and using books, they are unlikely to pass these skills on to their pupils. And then, however good the materials and the system that provides them might be, they are not used.

In Mali it was noted that, at the secondary level, neither teachers nor pupils had been trained in information skills. The training courses provided to those running the libraries were short and limited to organizational techniques.

It was concluded in Mozambique that teachers' own fear of books meant that they did little to encourage their use. They were also frightened that books which were used would be lost and therefore loans were restricted. In both projects, training of teachers in the use of book box libraries was considered insufficient. In the Ministry of Education (Mozambique) project, trainers did not pass on what they had learnt or circulate the guide on the use of book box libraries; indirect training did not work. An intermediate evaluation of the CODE project felt that objectives had not been reached because of the poor ability of primary school teachers to teach the early stages of reading. Success in introducing supplementary reading materials was linked to training primary school teachers in how to develop a better reading environment in their schools and communities. A new project component was therefore introduced aimed at improving the teaching of reading. As a result teachers began to be trained in the use of book box libraries to develop the oral tradition and the ability to tell stories in Portuguese and in methods of teaching reading and writing.

Although the Teachers Advisory Centre (Kenya) programme acknowledged the importance of training teachers who would be able to develop their pupils' reading abilities and to encourage independent learning and acquisition of good information skills, the TAC tutors were provided with no additional training and the researcher found that on the whole they lacked an information consciousness, resulting in the locking away of materials and the failure to assess the information needs of users.

In South Africa, the most successful READ schools were those with enthusiastic, motivated and committed teachers; those interviewed were unanimous that the teachers' role and attitude to the classroom library were crucial for maximizing access. Each teacher's creativity and ability to manipulate materials to suit each subject was critical to their use. Where classroom libraries were not used, this was often because teachers had reservations about departing from the traditional, more prescriptive methods of teaching and were reluctant to make use of books.

The READ programme gives as much emphasis on training as it does on the provision of materials; and this contributes greatly to the effectiveness of the classroom library model. Courses are provided at leadership, primary and high school levels, with as many follow-up sessions and workshops at the district level as are required. They concentrate on moving teachers from rote learning to the child-centred approach and on the development of professional skills, like those of language. The approach is resource-based and there are also courses in materials development, encouraging teachers to write new materials together with their pupils.

In none of the case studies were teachers much involved in the selection of materials, which is another way of increasing involvement and participation. Those interviewed in South Africa would have liked more direct consultation, rather than through the leader-teachers. They felt their experiences would be valuable to the process. In Kenya, the subject panels charged with the task of selection had long fallen into disuse and anyway there was no budget. Secondary schools in Mali also relied on donations, so selection was not applicable. The stock of Village Reading Rooms in Botswana was selected centrally by Library Service and teachers had no input.

Evidence that the key to the use of books lies in the training of the teachers comes from many other projects. The *Nueva Escuela* movement in Colombia and Guatemala (referred to in Chapter One) has at its heart the principle that teachers are facilitators of learning rather than disseminators of knowledge. It acknowledges that without on-going training, it is all too easy for teachers to revert to the old 'monologue' method of teaching. In Brazil, school libraries are seen as indispensable, but equally so is the training of teachers, so that they are encouraged to allow learners to build up their own knowledge and to participate in the educational process (Andrade Antunes, 1996).

A case study of a Teachers Resource Centre in Kenya (Munoko, 1996) gave the reactions of pupils to their teachers' lack of interest in the resources available. Pupils said that they liked the large variety of reading materials but complained about lack of encouragement in their use by teachers. The latter provided no feedback and were not positive. This led to the author recommending frequent in-service training of teachers, especially in appropriate integrated approaches and instructional techniques.

The impact of Ecole 2000 in Côte d'Ivoire was evaluated in 1995. One conclusion was that there was a need for more training of teachers and pupils in the use of books (Salzard and Cosson, 1996). The 1996 evaluation of the school library programme in Senegal of Aide et Action also concluded that teachers needed more involvement in using books as a tool. There was insufficient teaching with books. Children in early classes needed to be introduced to books through story telling, etc., even before they had learnt to read (Aide et Action, 1996).

The Children's Book Project (CBP) in Tanzania is an example of a programme that learnt from experience about the importance of training teachers. Started as a project to support the publishing in Kiswahili of books suitable for children, it has proved an effective vehicle for producing relevant and affordable local material (Minzi, 1999; Moshi, 1998; Mndambi, 1998). In the second phase six copies of each title published were distributed to six primary schools in around 117 districts countrywide, to provide nuclei of libraries. Instructions were included to assist teachers to set up these libraries. However CBP soon realized that distributing books to schools was only a beginning. It was also necessary to provide teachers with skills, so that they could guide pupils in getting the most out of the books. CBP is now involved in a three-year programme 'Language to Literacy' based on the READ model.

Support and monitoring

Also crucial to effectiveness is the support received at Government/Ministry, school and delivery level.

GOVERNMENT/MINISTRY SUPPORT

Education is a government responsibility and, whatever the model of information provision, it must have both the endorsement and the active support of government, especially that of the Ministry of Education or its equivalent. The major failure of the school library services in Ghana and Tanzania was that they failed to convince educational planners and administrators that school libraries were a necessity and not a luxury. In Ghana, official interest was said throughout to be cool and casual rather than active and sustained. In Kenya, there has never been any official policy towards school libraries, which has resulted in piecemeal development.

The history of school level provision in Africa has shown how the conflict over who is responsible – the Ministry (and which Ministry) or the national public library service – has been a weakening factor. When responsibility is split it is all too easy to blame the other partner for service break-down. In Botswana, for example, responsibility for library provision in schools is split between the National Library Service and the Ministry of Education, with the former providing library staff in senior secondary schools and the latter in junior secondary schools. Thus, although libraries have been provided in all such schools, provision of an adequate service cannot be assured. There is the same sort of situation in Tanzania. Tanzania Library Service (TLS) has a mandate to set up school libraries, but has no powers to set up and administer budgets or insist that funds are provided. There is a lack of formal co-ordination and liaison mechanisms between TLS and the operational and planning departments in the Ministry. Although there is a Libraries Co-ordinator post in the Ministry, it has no formal connection with TLS. Existence of such a post merely allows the Ministry to pay lip service to the importance of libraries in schools, but at the same time to avoid any real commitment to their development.

Evidence suggests that it is best when just one agency in government is responsible for school book provision and that it is located within the Ministry of Education. Only then do libraries stand a chance of being integrated into the whole process of education. In Ghana, the fact that the school library service emanated from the public library system was seen as a weakness, despite the professional competency it promised. Momentum had to come from the Ministry of Education and therefore any School Library Service also had to be located there. In Botswana, the only way to ensure that school libraries worked hand in hand with the school curriculum was seen to be the setting up of a school library service in the Ministry of Education to oversee development (Jorosi, 1997).

National school curricula also need to be resource-based, if educational materials provided are to be used effectively. In South Africa where the proposed new curriculum is outcomes-based, there is a new attitude towards the provision of learning resources. Where once the entire education system was characterized by a lack of understanding of the relevance of learning resources, now educators need to be familiar with such resources and how they can be used and learners need to acquire the skills to source, access and manipulate information. Those interviewed during the research reported that the Department of Education officials were totally supportive of classroom libraries and READ programmes. In fact the DoE wants READ's work to expand and an official report recommended that it service all nine provinces of South Africa. Official attitudes to education are changing throughout Africa (as indicated in Chapter Two), but in many countries the learning process remains textbook and teacher-orientated. It is therefore not surprising that one primary school head teacher in Tanzania made the following comment on the available supplementary reading materials: 'I can't use the reading books because they don't follow the curriculum' (Buchan, 1995).

Legislation and standards are often seen by librarians as being the ultimate expression of government support to school book provision. Sometimes these do work, as in Botswana, where the present network of school libraries and Village Reading Rooms, has resulted from the 1994 Revised National Policy on Education. But equally they can do as much harm as good. In Tanzania the legislation is there. There is the *TLS Board Act* of 1975, plus the *School Library Resource Centre Regulations* of 1986 and the *1987 Standards and Manual for School and College Libraries in Tanzania*. But implementation has not followed good intentions. In fact the *Regulations* are far removed from the reality of the situation in Tanzania and the *Manual* again sets very unrealistic standards for space, stock and staffing. It can be argued that such legislation has prevented school level book provision, that is within the financial resources currently available in Tanzania, from taking place.

One way of giving official recognition to library and book provision would be to certify courses taken by teachers. This was raised in South Africa. Those interviewed suggested that certification could be awarded after a number of training sessions, a certification that would be recognized by education authorities and rewarded. It would become a part of career progression. This would be an incentive for all teachers to become involved and would result in more teachers being motivated to give READ programmes the seriousness and attention they deserve.

SCHOOL SUPPORT

At the school level, principals and heads need to be committed to the system of book provision. Without this, teachers are not encouraged to use the materials, attend workshops, etc. In Mozambique, it was found that, without this support, school timetables did not have provision for library periods. In Kenya, school transport was not made available for teachers to visit TACs nor school subscriptions paid. In Mali the numbers of staff needed to run the library were not provided. A centralized school library service was of no use at all, if the schools themselves did not first establish libraries.

The case study from South Africa provides the most convincing evidence in this respect. Lack of support from school principals was identified as one of the biggest problems. Not only were teachers not encouraged to attend training workshops, but sometimes their classes had to be cancelled and they had to meet their own costs (which could be considerable for those in rural schools). In addition, it caused a lack of continuity both between classes and between schools. One teacher's diligence could be nullified by the next class. What was needed here was a whole-school monitoring policy, to ensure the effective use of class libraries throughout the school. And such a policy could only emanate from the principal. READ has acknowledged this problem and has begun courses in school governance.

Evidence on the importance of the attitude of a headteacher also comes from other research. For a writer from Nigeria (Adekanmbi, 1998) winning the support of primary school headteachers and proprietors was seen as the only way forward to developing book provision at this level. She therefore began workshops to equip such people with library skills. In many African schools, parents pay a levy towards supplementary reading materials provision. However it is rarely used for that purpose. In Kenya, in Kisumu, parents of primary school pupils each pay KSh50/- per year (around 80 US cents) towards TAC activities. However headteachers do not remit these funds to the TAC and, since donor funding ended in 1996, no new reading materials have been purchased (Kramiller and Fairhurst, 1999). In Cameroon, a sum of money (again around 80 US cents) is collected from each pupil at primary and secondary level for the purpose of library development (Balock, 1997). It is not known how the money is used. It could be that, as stated by McGregor and others in reference to Kenya (1990), most headteachers lack guidance on how to build and maintain a library – guidance on useful titles and on appropriate storage and maintenance.

Teachers need on-going support from the modality itself. They have to feel that their work is being given due recognition, their needs are being addressed and their day-to-day problems solved. This is the sort of support that a school library service gives, when it is run efficiently. Those interviewed in South Africa congratulated READ in this respect. A back-up of a network of leader-teachers and library advisers is available in each district. Teachers emphasized that this support was only 'a telephone call away'. The team spirit nurtured by READ also means that support is readily available from colleagues. The good interpersonal relations between READ library advisers and teachers was stressed, as well as the flexibility of the programme. Changes were made on request (for instance in the number of books per library) and workshops arranged whenever needed. Mutual respect and appreciation was the order of the day. Evaluation was in-built in the programme.

This type of on-going support was not always available in the other modalities. In Mali, school librarians worked very much in isolation and library users, both teachers and pupils, were critical of their abilities in managing information. It was the view of the researcher that TAC tutors in Kenya would need extensive training if they were to be able to create that atmosphere of cordiality and customer care needed to motivate teachers to use centres. They would have to be able to evaluate their collections and their relevance to the needs of the school population. For two of the book box systems established in Mozambique, the aim was to circulate the boxes and thus increase the numbers and variety of materials available. But the mobile libraries project concluded that there was not much understanding about receiving and despatching boxes, whilst that organized by Action Nord Sud decided that the human resources available (coupled with the lack of transport) would necessitate that the libraries became static in the future. The supervision given to Village Reading Rooms from BNLS branch libraries was 'occasional'. Staff working in the reading rooms were generally primary school leavers and therefore did not have the level of education or training to assist teachers in their work.

Book accessibility, availability and relevance

ACCESSIBILITY

The objective of providing supplementary reading materials is to ensure that books are integrated with learning. It stands to reason that close proximity and constant access to books is likely to have the best results. Books need to 'saturate' the learning process. If books are at hand then pupils will be able to read whenever they have a free moment and teachers will be able to pick up a book to illustrate a point. On the spot accessibility promotes greater use of resources, independent learning and the reading habit.

In this respect the classroom library provides the best accessibility. It is open for both teacher and pupil use at every hour of the school day. Since it is located in the classroom it is near at hand and children can make use of books for many lessons during the school week. Queries raised and problems posed may be dealt with by teacher and pupil acting together at the time the need arises. Books are not hidden away in a locked cupboard or in a separate room, but can be there in the classroom on desks, tables and display racks.

In the other case studies, access proved to be a source of complaint or a factor limiting impact. The secondary school libraries of Mali were only open during class hours – when pupils were in class. In Mozambique, the teacher in charge of the book box also taught, so the books were locked away from those not in his/her class most of the time. Statistics showed few visits per pupil were made. A visit to a TAC collection in Kenya might necessitate a journey of 10 km or more. Once a Village Reading Room in Botswana moved out of its primary school location, class use dropped off, indicating that such relocation actually reduced many students use of and familiarity with library facilities and supplementary reading materials.

The school library project managed by Aide et Action (1996) in Senegal found that keeping books centrally in one classroom limited accessibility. As a result of its evaluation, a new system of book suitcases managed by classes was instituted. Instead of the child going to the book, the book would come to the child.

AVAILABILITY AND RELEVANCE

It is also important that the number of books available are sufficient for the numbers of teachers and pupils served and that the books are relevant to what is taught and up to date.

It is frequently argued that only the school or community library, because of its potential size, can meet these criteria, especially when it is run by a professionally trained librarian and backed by a school library service, which can provide supplementary material for special projects. Certainly those interviewed in Botswana considered the existing materials (around 2.5 books per pupil) to be useful and effective for primary school work, although lacking in certain areas like computers and local language publications. However, the fact that selection was done centrally and by a section where frequent staff changes meant that little experience was built up about VRR needs at the primary level, was thought to limit relevance. Similarly one of the secondary school libraries in Mali did provide the best ratio of books per pupil, nearly 5.

However, teachers and pupils were still dissatisfied and 80% claimed that readers' information needs could only be met by increasing and improving the collection; in particular journal subscriptions were required.

The numbers of books provided through the book box libraries (around 0.1 per pupil in the MINED project and 1.5 in that of CODE in Mozambique) were definitely insufficient. Interested pupils and quick readers had to wait. The same is likely to be true for basic level school libraries in Mali, which will offer 0.85 books per pupil. The books in all these projects have been selected by experts, so relevance is high. The MINED project offered three different book boxes, by level and according to whether a school was urban or rural. But in Mozambique there were still some complaints that not all the books provided were appropriate. The most sought after were the imported four-colour publications with good illustrations; the texts of those produced locally were often long and difficult. The TAC collections in Kenya were sufficient neither in numbers nor relevance. A frequent comment of teachers interviewed was that the materials were not sufficient and were irrelevant to their needs. Not all subjects of the primary school curriculum were covered.

That relevance is as important as availability comes from the READ case study in South Africa. Each classroom library has a minimum of 60 books (around 1.7 per pupil) but the number can be increased and those interviewed usually managed libraries of around 120 books. Fast readers are catered for by borrowing from a library serving the next higher class in the school. Each library is carefully selected and graded, so that it meets the demands of the curriculum. The responsiveness of the selection policy to expressed needs, is evidenced by the way READ now includes fiction with mixed settings, rather than restricting stories to those with black African backgrounds.

Classroom libraries and book box libraries have been said to be restrictive and to act as a barrier to pupils moving on to the use of larger collections and to exploring other sources of information. The findings of the South African case study negate this argument. Whilst the teachers agreed that the classroom library was not sufficient for teaching all library skills to both pupils and teachers, it did provide a stepping stone to larger collections. Some of the teachers took their pupils to public libraries in town and block borrowed materials to enrich their classroom collections. In one school, some of the classroom libraries had been collapsed to form a central school library, which ran alongside the individual classroom libraries. There is no evidence to suggest that classroom libraries are any less or more restrictive than the VRRs of Botswana, which are already part of a larger national public library system.

Role of NGOs

Education may be the ultimate responsibility of government, but the case studies reveal the increasingly important role NGOs are playing in book provision at the school level. This role is not merely restricted to initiating and financing projects but encompasses day to day management. And increasingly NGOs do not work alone but in partnership with both government and other NGOs.

Examples are many, coming from both the case studies and other projects. The local NGO READ manages the classroom libraries in South Africa. In Mozambique, whilst CODE, a Canadian NGO, provided the finance for the 'portable' libraries project, Progresso, a local NGO, was contracted to act as co-ordinator and manager. Bibliothèque–Lecture–Développment (BLD), a local NGO in Senegal, works with Ministry of Education blessing and has been mostly supported by CODE in its 'installing libraries' programme. Many of the French Co-operation projects in Francophone Africa are partnerships between France, the government of the country concerned and both local and French NGOs. The first phase of South African Book Aid Project (SABAP) in 1998 was implemented on a partnership basis. The Eastern Cape Department of Education through the Provincial Libraries and Information Service (PLIS) Directorate was the owner of the project; Book Aid International (BAI) managed it at the British end; it was implemented by a local NGO, the Institute of Training and Education for Capacity Building (ITEC), working in partnership with PLIS. Finance came from the Department For International Development (DFID) UK.

Advantages that NGOs have over government ministries are:
- They are able to raise funds from all kinds of sources, ones that are perhaps not easily tapped by government. For example, READ relies very much on the private sector in South Africa for funding. In Kenya, where school provision is the sole responsibility of government, this source has not been tapped, although two-thirds of the GDP is accounted for by private enterprise. Funders often find NGOs more directly accountable than large government ministries. READ has managed to maintain its same funders over many years.
- They are more flexible in the ways they can operate. They can support local initiatives, as in Mozambique, rather than concentrate on the whole country situation. Decision-making is speedy. They adjust their staffing levels and expertise to the jobs in hand. There is no danger of staffing levels being maintained when the work or the finance for the work

has disappeared, as has happened in the school library services of Ghana and Tanzania.

At the same time it is important that government still provide overall support, co-ordination and control at the national level. Once there is NGO involvement, there is a danger that national Ministries or Departments of Education abrogate their responsibilities towards school level provision.

- Short-term and one-off provision of reading books is not the same thing as creating a sustainable service, providing a regular and maintainable collection of reading books in a school. The 'institutionalization' of what has been an NGO project into the national education system can also prove difficult.

The researcher in Mozambique has pointed out that whilst there is a school libraries section in the Ministry, this has no policy and is without financial and human resources to function properly. The lack of a strong co-ordinating agency means that there has been a poor exchange of information between the various 'library' projects operating in the country. Previous experiences are not therefore used as a basis to move forward.

The government in South Africa is anxious that READ continue its programmes and expand them, into new districts and into high schools. But READ operates under financial constraints. It needs some financial support from the DoE to undertake new assignments. Teachers who wanted to replenish their libraries in the middle of the school year, also thought that DoE could provide some financial support for this purpose.

The evaluation of phase 1 of SABAP (1998) has indicated that PLIS does not have a strong sense of ownership and control of the project.

- The introduction of curricula favouring book-based learning must also be the responsibility of government, as is recognition of courses for teachers related to the use of libraries, such as those run by READ.

Local publishing industries

A corollary of any strategy to provide supplementary reading materials is local book production. Book and library development go hand in hand. Cultural context, language, interests and purpose must all be taken into account when books are selected for children. Such books need both to reflect the lives of children and to take them outside and beyond their immediate environment, opening windows onto other worlds. 'A wide variety of different

book types and genres, including fiction and non-fiction, is necessary to give children an orientation in the rich world of literature
as well as opportunities to experience and select according to needs
and preferences, and to make reading a purposeful activity' (Hugo,
1998). Books which are written and created with the children of a
particular country in mind are required. Only local publishing can
meet this need.

Many of the case studies (for example Ghana and Kenya)
revealed the belief that until there was a viable local publishing
industry producing relevant materials, in sufficient quantities and
at realistic prices, then provision of supplementary materials to the
school population would always be disadvantaged. Frequently, as
in Botswana, it was local language material that was lacking.

That major advances have been made in the 1990s in
autonomous publishing in Africa has already been indicated in
Chapter Two. There the growth in children's publishing has been
described (Faye, 1998). The experiences of one publisher in Kenya
were presented to the Zimbabwe International Book Fair at the
1998 Indaba (Chakava, 1998). Many funding agencies have been
supportive in this area. Examples are: Agence de Coopération
Culturelle et Technique, which has two support programmes
encouraging the development of the book publishing industry in
Francophone Africa; Bellagio Publishing Network, an informal
association of funding agencies and other organizations dedicated
to the strengthening of indigenous publishing since 1991; and
CODE, which has been the initiator of such programmes as the
previously mentioned Children's Book Project in Tanzania. As of
1998, Children's Book Project (Tanzania) had published 132 titles
in print runs of 5,000. The NGO READ, faced with the problem of
finding good quality, attractive and culturally sensitive books to
put in classrooms in South Africa, began its own book development and publication programme.

That said, progress in local publishing of children's books is
patchy. Some countries do better than others. Unit costs of
publishing reading books are much higher than for textbooks,
because of smaller print runs and the need for a large number of
titles. When minority languages are used, costs are even higher. A
thesis written in 1994 (Konaté Sié) looked at children's literature in
Burkina Faso, Côte d'Ivoire and Senegal. Publishers only put a
small proportion of their budget (an average of 0.02%) to the publication of supplementary reading materials. Another analysis
(Gazza, 1997) estimates that in 1993 children's literature in Africa
formed only 2% of local production. Whereas 40% of the population in Francophone Africa are children, only 5% of the production
is for children. Just not enough books are being published.

162   However evidence from the case studies suggests that once library systems of some sort are in place, then publishing at the local level develops to meet the market needs. In Mali 18.4% of the books going to basic schools are published in Mali. In Mozambique, the CODE project by the fourth and fifth year had moved towards almost total acquisition of books produced locally. In Kenya, there is already a strong local publishing industry that operates under capacity. If the library market was there, then more books would be published.

Community involvement

In countries which have not yet developed a culture of reading and an appreciation of literacy, it is necessary to supplement access to books in schools with programmes which encourage support of reading in the wider community. The *Nueva Escuela* movement has this at the heart of its programmes – the integration of the school in the community and the community in the school. SABAP also has as one of its four goals 'improved community understanding of the importance of books'.

This understanding can be attained by encouraging parental involvement. Parents are important role models in literacy activities. Literacy should occur as a part of everyday family life. Parents need to provide opportunities and resources and interact with their children during the reading process. One important aspect of this process is to send books home regularly with children. Parental involvement is a strong feature of the READ programmes; its philosophy is that the reading habit cannot be sustained with success without collaborative effort between pupils, teachers and parents. Community resource centres should be strong in this respect, as the library is used by the whole community. However this was not evidenced by the VRR case study in Botswana. Most models allow home loan, although in many cases this was low and restricted because of fears that books would be lost or damaged.

Motivational programmes and literacy campaigns are also important to community appreciation. Reading can be promoted through such activities as book fairs, book days, festivals, story telling, reading clubs, story writing competitions at national, regional and local levels. Worth mentioning is the work done by La Joie par les Livres (JPL) and the Council for Children's Science Publications in Africa (CHICSI). JPL, through its Intercultural Section set up in 1986, co-ordinates the work of all those who want to promote children's reading in Francophone Africa. CHICSI was founded in 1988 with a mandate to stimulate and promote publishing and ownership of reading materials by and for children. Its programme includes mobile reading tents, workshops and establishment of libraries. It organizes the Pan-African Children's

Book Fair and in 1998 started a children's home library campaign (Bugembe, 1998).

READ's classroom libraries are supported by two major motivational programmes, also organized by READ. One is the READathon, an annual national campaign which culminates on International Literacy Day and is celebrated in all school and educational facilities throughout the country, with the active involvement and participation of local communities. The other is the nationwide annual Festival of Books, a competition of dramatized performances of selected children's stories and poetry.

Infrastructure

For books to reach schools demands a functioning transport and communications infrastructure. This is especially important when books are rotated between schools, as in some of the book box systems. Such an infrastructure cannot always be guaranteed in Africa.

The researcher in Botswana noted that it was Botswana's relatively good internal communications – a network of tarred roads, fuel supplies, regular bus and air services, a system of government vehicles – that allowed the National Library Service to service the VRRs. In addition, Botswana's ever-expanding primary school building programme ensured the existence of buildings in which to house VRRs. In Mozambique, lack of transport and poor roads meant that circulating book box libraries were a non-starter. Transport and communication problems in Kenya also impaired access to TACs by teachers in the surrounding areas.

Costs and cost-effectiveness

'In the final analysis, the whole problem of library services in the developing world comes down to the cost of the service and the need to make it as cost-effective as possible' (Doust, 1998). Any government in Africa will want to choose the cheapest possible option of providing supplementary reading materials, so long as the method is effective and achieves the necessary impact.

Costs

Throughout the case studies, the researchers have indicated that data on costs was not easy to find. However, from the evidence provided, some estimates of cost per pupil have been made. These mostly refer to set-up costs. Direct comparisons between the estimates are problematic, as variables such as the number of books provided need to be taken into account. However the calculations do give some indication of the relative costs of the different models.

School library services

- School library services were not costed. However these can only supplement the library that is already established and maintained by the school. Costs will therefore be additional to the ones incurred in setting up and running the school library. Those examined appeared to have become an expensive and not very effective additional layer of bureaucracy.

School libraries

- In Mali, the libraries being provided to basic level schools cost in the region of US$3,000 each, i.e. about US$10 per pupil. This figure includes the purchase cost of the books (just over 50%); the rest is spent in training librarians and creating, equipping and operating the management structure in the Ministry. It does not include the cost of the library premises or the staff. The first library to open cost in the region of US$2,000 to build and equip; costs per pupil could therefore be in the region of US$17.
- The literature provides a more complete costing of fixed libraries in primary schools in Bulawayo, Zimbabwe (Doust, 1998). This estimate is very much higher than the one worked out for Mali. It is calculated that it would cost a total of US$8,288 to build and equip a library room, provide 2,000 books, maintain the premises and staff with one part-time librarian. Given an average of 100 pupils per school, this works out at US$83 per pupil.
- The secondary school libraries in Mali were not costed. However it was pointed out that they could not become effective unless they were run by professional librarians, housed in purpose built or specially adapted premises and offered adequate annual budgets to purchase the books and journals required to meet user needs.

The cost of a school library will always be high because of the need for separate premises and specially trained library staff.

Classroom libraries

- The cost of one READ classroom library has been estimated at US$313.50 and the cost per school at US$4,702.50. This works out around US$9 per pupil. This figure does not include any administrative or training costs. In other modalities examined these usually work out at around 50% of the total cost. Therefore in South Africa, the cost per pupil is likely to be in the region of US$18.

- Similar costs were incurred in the first phase of SABAP (although the books supplied under this scheme do not necessarily form classroom libraries). Taking the total cost of the project, deducting the cost of purchasing and processing books for non-school libraries, and then dividing this figure by the number of schools (200) and the average number of pupils in each school (108), gives a cost of US$16 per pupil.

A big advantage of the classroom library is that it does not require any special premises or equipment (the existing classroom is its home). In addition it does not require the post of a professional teacher-librarian. The existing class teacher acts in this role. For South Africa, this is important. Expenditure cutbacks have targeted school libraries and have caused the withdrawal of full-time qualified teacher-librarians. The latter are no longer included in teacher/pupil ratios and schools need to raise extra funds, if they are to be employed.

Book box libraries

- The book box libraries of Mozambique cost between US$0.12 (at the initial level of the MINED project) and US$2.75 (in the CODE project) per pupil. This was for the whole service, including the cost of books, training and administration.
- A proposed book box project for Tanzania (Carpenter and Kemp, 1989) came up with higher estimates. The cost per school of providing boxes for each grade (and including book purchase and administrative costs of 50%) was estimated to be in the region of US$2,130. With an average of 280 pupils per school, this worked out at US$7.6 per pupil. In this scheme, 2.5 books were allowed per pupil.

Teachers Resource Centres

- Although costs of the TAC collections in Kenya were not available in the case study, a subsequent memo from the TAC tutor in Eldoret provided a break down (Nawatsi, 1997). The set up costs of equipment and books, plus the annual costs of staff salaries and stationery, totalled US$14,683, working out at US$0.7 per pupil.

Community Resource Centres

- The average stock of a VRR in Botswana is around 2,311 books. 60% of the stock is estimated to be for children and, given an average cost of US$7 per book, the stock would have cost US$9,709. However in the sampled VRRs, the stock had been built up over a period of 12 years, giving an average expenditure of US$809 per year. If 50% is added for administrative costs, this works out at US$2.7 per pupil per year.

Cost-effectiveness

There is no direct relation between costs and cost-effectiveness; the most expensive models of book provision are not necessarily the most effective, nor the cheapest the least effective. It really depends on what the cost covers – the level of teacher involvement and support, the accessibility, availability and relevance of the books provided. For example, school libraries are expensive, but unless there is a budget to purchase new materials regularly and professional library staff to provide the organization and service, users are not satisfied. TACs are low in cost per pupil, but the materials held are inadequate in number and access is difficult. Book boxes are economic but give limited access and choice of titles.

Any model of book delivery also has some impact on pupil performance. The presence of supplementary reading materials, especially when no other source is available, has a positive effect. However to relate this impact to the cost and level of provision is difficult, without also comparing the progress of children in control schools. Such an exercise has only been carried out in READ schools, where it was concluded that language proficiency increased by up to two years in those schools operating classroom libraries.

Funding partnerships

One way of reducing the costs borne by any one party is to set up funding partnerships. The role of NGOs has already been discussed. In Botswana the costs of VRRs are shared between government ministries. Another approach is to ask the community to cost share. In Mali at the level of basic provision, the local population provided the premises, furniture and shelves of each school library. In Botswana, the Village Development Committees provide free standing premises. Some schools levy library fees on students. Those interviewed in Tanzania thought that school libraries would have to rely more on parental contributions in the future. The willingness of parents and communities to provide financial support depends to a great extent on how much they are involved in and appreciate the role of books in education and learning.

READ has led the way in partnerships with the private business sector, arguing that business and industries cannot optimize their operations when the majority of their work force is illiterate. These partnerships can involve direct financial support as well as indirect, such as providing venues, transportation or the use of equipment and labour.

Reliance on funding from various sources may cause problems. The researcher from Botswana has pointed out that this involves long-term collaboration and commitment, perhaps resulting in conflicts of interest and in possible inertia. Responsibility may be too diffused.

Costs and Gross National Product

How much a country can afford to spend on supplementary reading provision will depend on the general wealth of the country concerned. This will determine not only the amount of the government contribution but also that of parents, if cost-sharing is introduced. In Africa, economic conditions between countries vary considerably, as is shown by the following table (World Bank), which relates to the countries of the case studies. Because of this, not all countries will want or be able to take the same path of book provision.

Table 9.1 GNP *per capita* in 1998

Country	US$
Botswana	3020
Ghana	360
Kenya	320
Mali	280
Mozambique	80
South Africa	3520
Tanzania	170

Sustainability

Most of the models examined in the case studies are dependent on funding agencies to some extent. Only the VRRs in Botswana are maintained by government funding. (The MINED book box project in Mozambique was funded by the national budget, but this took place in the early 1980s.) School library services are still funded nationally, but that funding is mostly restricted to staff salaries and the books distributed are normally donations. The libraries for the basic schools in Mali are paid for by the French government, those at the secondary level rely on donations to augment their collections. READ raises all its funds, albeit mostly locally and from the private sector. The portable library project in Mozambique was completely funded by CODE. TACs in Kenya have not received acquisition budgets from the Ministry for the last five to six years; the material they have came on donation, mostly received from DFID.

The danger of relying on donor funding is that when it ceases, so does book provision. Serious consideration has to be given in the design of a project to the levels of support that can be afforded and will be committed within the country concerned, whether this support will come from government or the community. READ has found an answer by starting partnerships with the private sector. But not all countries have a private sector that is as well developed as that of South Africa. The levels of possible parental or community contributions are unlikely to be sufficient for the replacement of books year after year, especially in countries with a low GNP. Yet many African governments would now like to pass this burden over to parents, restricting their own contribution to the upkeep of premises and staff salaries.

Which model?

An indication of the strengths of the models examined in the case studies is given in Table 9. 2.

Table 9.2 Strengths of different school library models

	SLS	School Library	Classroom Library	Book box Library	TAC	VRR
Teacher involvement			√			
Ongoing support	√		√	√		√
Accessibility			√			
Availability and relevance		√	√	√		√
Low cost			√	√	√	√

School library services

School library services (SLSs) can and do raise awareness about the need for school libraries, provide advice and training in their organization and management and improve availability and relevance, through assistance in selection and supply of materials.

The major drawback is that, first of all, school libraries have to exist in each school for the service to be of benefit. It is therefore an add-on and increases the costs of school book provision. As an add-on it is an expensive option. Countries like Ghana and Tanzania, which are no longer able to maintain libraries in schools, therefore also fail to fund their school library services.

Another drawback is that SLSs which emanate from a public library service (as they do in Ghana and Tanzania), whilst being strong on library organization, lack teacher involvement and ways of integrating provision of books into teacher training courses. Co-ordination between the public library service and the Ministry of Education proves difficult to maintain. The evidence suggests that it is better for SLSs to be financed, organized and controlled by a Ministry of Education.

Even in the developed world, SLSs have an uncertain future. The UK government has decided to end the central funding of SLSs by local education authorities (Library Association Record, 1998). Instead individual schools are to control their own budgets and buy back into a SLS only if they wish. It is thought that not all schools will want to buy back and that those that do will opt for a reduced subscription. SLSs are unlikely to be sustainable.

That said, in African countries which have opted to develop traditional school libraries, SLSs are still seen as a way of raising standards. Eritrea runs a SLS from within its Ministry of Education. This is even considering introducing a centralized cataloguing and processing service (Berhane, 1996; Field, 1999). In Botswana, the setting up of a SLS in the Ministry of Education is seen as a way to develop the libraries that exist and strengthen their role in the learning process. Without it, libraries are seen as being marginalized (Jorosi, 1997). If traditional school libraries are chosen as the way forward, then it would seem that a SLS is necessary to maintain standards and encourage development.

School libraries

Centralized school libraries are often viewed in Africa as the 'right' solution, partly because this is a Western model and anything else is thought to be substandard. The major advantage of school libraries is that stocks can be built up over many years, providing greater availability and relevance, and that their size justifies the employment of professional librarians and purpose-built premises.

But these features are not always present in school libraries. In one of Mali's secondary schools, the greater availability of books did not bring satisfaction, because of lack of relevance. Staff were poorly trained (mostly having received just one two-week course in organizational techniques) and the collections were not housed in purpose-built or specially adapted premises. In short, the libraries were proving too expensive to establish and maintain. In addition accessibility proved to be a problem. The libraries were only open during class hours – when pupils were in class; the hours also tended to be irregular. At one school over 60% of those questioned complained about times of opening.

Extending school libraries throughout a country is also a daunting prospect, given their cost. In South Africa (where the official policy is that every educational institution should have its own library) only 17% of schools at present have libraries. This means that 22,550 schools need to have libraries built, equipped and maintained. Mali has chosen the road of setting up a library in each of its basic schools. However there are almost 2,000 of these schools and only 10 were included in the first phase of the library programme, with 20 planned in the second. It will take many, many years before the programme reaches completion.

Another problem with school libraries is that their role within a school has never been properly defined and accepted by teachers. If they are to aid classroom learning, then the library needs to be at the heart of the curriculum. If they are to provide creative reading for pleasure, stimulation and extension of language skills, then teachers need more knowledge of books. If they are to provide opportunities for a child's personal development, then teachers must put aside time for them to be used. If libraries are to be integrated into the learning process, then it must be teachers who define this role, not librarians. Resource-based teaching and school libraries do not go hand in hand.

Classroom libraries

Classroom libraries, as run by READ in South Africa, meet most of the criteria that lead to effective book provision.

There is strong teacher involvement and commitment. This partly arises from the training programme organized by READ in the use of books in the learning process. But it is also the result of teachers having immediate and day-to-day control over the way their libraries are organized and used.

READ provides a network of support to those in charge of the classroom libraries. Leader-teachers and library advisers are available in each district, just 'a telephone call away'. READ has also won the support of the Department of Education officials and has begun courses in school governance, to win over the support of school principals.

Because classroom libraries are in the classroom, they are always accessible by teachers and pupils, during the teaching-learning process. Home loans are allowed, except for Grades 1 and 2.

Although the number of books per pupil is usually smaller than in a school library, the number can be increased and those interviewed usually managed libraries of around 120 books. Fast readers are catered for by borrowing from a library serving the next highest class in the school. Relevance is high, as books are selected for their bearing on the curriculum of that class and the age of the class.

READ also campaigns to strengthen the reading culture and parental and community involvement.

Costs are moderate, with little demand on staff or premises. No extra room is required, as the classroom is the location. No extra staff are required, as the class teacher is also the person in charge. Private sector funding is raised and has now been sustained over a number of years.

Whether the READ model of classroom libraries can be transferred elsewhere in Africa is yet to be proven, although projects are now underway in Tanzania, Lesotho and Nigeria. The first phase of SABAP has some similarities, although not all of its book collections find their way to classroom libraries. The evaluation (SABAP, 1998) raised a number of questions. Although teachers were fairly positive, learners were less so. 54% of learners claimed that the books were too difficult and 76% said that they had not borrowed in the past two weeks. 60% of schools did not allow home loans. It was obviously quite difficult to get the levels of the materials right. The fact that emphasis was placed on training teachers in library routines rather than in the use of books could also have had an effect. There were also indications that management might be problematic in the future. Unlike READ, which has always been in sole charge of development, SABAP was implemented on a partnership basis. The handover from the main implementing NGO, ITEC, to the eventual owner, the Provincial Libraries and Information Service, was not proving to be easy, in that the transfer of relevant knowledge and skills had not led PLIS to feel that it now owned and controlled the project.

Book box libraries

The major advantage of book box libraries is their low cost. The boxes can be used anywhere, needing no physical facilities at all. In rural areas this is especially important, as many schools operate under trees. The box can be used in the open air and then returned to a teacher's home at night. Because the number of books in a box is small, within the school it can be managed by a teacher with a minimum of training. At the same time the supply of books has a positive impact on pupil skills.

However, as it has already been pointed out earlier in this

chapter, the research in Mozambique showed that without instituting a programme of training for teachers parallel to the provision of book boxes, the resources were little used. Accessibility also proved a problem. Although books were present in the school, they were not necessarily available to a class, resulting in low usage. Because books were specially chosen by experts, relevance was high. But because the numbers of books are limited to those in the box, availability per pupil was low. In Mozambique, interested pupils and quick readers had to wait.

By circulating book boxes between schools, it is possible to increase the numbers and the variety of materials available. But this demands a strong support system, plus a good communications and transport infrastructure. In Mozambique, it was found that circulating book boxes did not work. It was difficult to engender an understanding about receiving and despatching boxes and this, coupled with the lack of transport and poor roads, necessitated that libraries would become static in the future.

Similar conclusions were reached in an evaluation of a book box loan scheme organized in Kenya through TACs in the early 1990s. 40 boxes of books were distributed to schools in 470 zonal areas and the boxes were to circulate between schools. Although most teachers said that the use of the books improved pupils' language skills, a lack of knowledge was revealed on how to manage the books. Only one box was received by each school, which meant that the books were neither adequate nor suitable for all classes. In most schools, use was restricted to one library period per week (35 minutes). Only about half of the teachers had been given any training in the use of the books. Although it had been intended that the scheme would be maintained through fees from the loaning schools, this plan was not successful. Much more support and monitoring was required from TAC tutors.

A book box scheme has been provided to primary schools in rural areas of Botswana since 1976, organized by the National Library Service. An evaluation in 1992 (SIAPAC-Africa) raised the same sort of issues. Teachers and pupils were positive about the impact of being able to access supplementary reading materials and most felt that the selection (with some reservations about subject matter and level) was good. However usage was not high – only 26.3% of pupils had used the book box at least once in the year under investigation. Access could be difficult – the boxes tended not to be used in classroom situations and often the book box room was closed after school and at weekends, when pupils wanted to consult books. Teachers tended to use the materials more for leisure than for teaching. And use was limited by disinterest amongst the teachers who did not use the boxes at all (about half) and by lack of encouragement from parents. Obviously the use of books needed to be better integrated with the curriculum and more community involvement was required.

Teachers Advisory Centres

TACS may be a low cost alternative, but they have little impact. In theory, the TAC programme acknowledges the importance of training teachers who would be able to develop their pupils' reading abilities and to encourage independent learning and acquisition of good information skills. In practice, the TAC tutors are provided with no additional training and the researcher found that, on the whole, they lacked an information consciousness, resulting in the locking away of materials and the failure to assess the information needs of users.

Access to TAC collections was a major problem. The books were not available in the schools, but a journey's distance away. The hours TACs were open were very irregular and usually not more than two days each week. Information on what materials were available was not circulated. Even if a teacher found a TAC open, loaning material was not allowed. Only 20% of teachers interviewed had visited their TAC to source materials. In addition TAC collections were sufficient neither in numbers nor relevance.

A survey of Teachers Resource Centres (TRCs) (the Kenyan equivalent at secondary level of TACs) in Uasin Gishu District in 1992 revealed the same drawbacks. 50% of the schools sampled were members, but usage in these was not high. It was the opportunity to borrow book boxes and class sets that was most appreciated. The main problems raised were the distance of schools from the TRC and the inability (or unwillingness) of head teachers to pay the membership fee. In addition many teachers were unaware of the functions and existence of the TRC. More motivational programmes by TRC tutors could have increased usage and impact.

A wider survey of TRCs in Kenya, Zambia, Nepal and India (Kramiller and Fairhurst, 1999) examined (amongst other aspects) the effectiveness of TRCs in transferring resources and materials to schools. The overall conclusion was that TRCs were neither successful as a 'library' of reference materials nor as a depot for loaning books and teaching/learning materials. In addition, they were not sustainable, remaining reliant on donors for funds and ideas. A major problem was that TRCs were detached from schools and therefore little used. However the book box schemes of TACs and TRCs in Kenya, led the study to suggest that there may be a future for TRCs, if they became centres for school-based resourcing. They should focus on getting learning materials into the hands of pupils in classrooms, i.e. become centres for the organization of classroom and book box library schemes. Once the books were in the schools, then teachers could be trained in how to support the use of the learning materials by pupils.

Village Reading Rooms

The success of Village Reading Rooms in meeting the supplementary reading material needs of primary school pupils has been something of an accident. Village Reading Rooms were set up primarily to support the needs of post-literates. In the event they have been used mostly by school pupils. And those interviewed felt that English language skills, in particular, had increased and that there was an improvement in school-leaving examination results in pupils who regularly used the facility. Costs were kept low by sharing physical facilities, stock and staff with the whole community. The provision of stock centrally by BNLS had ensured maximum discounts. Various government ministries shared in funding the programme.

However the researcher indicated that problems exist. Because adult users disliked the location of the library in a primary school, there had been a move to use separate free-standing buildings. This has reduced class use of the books. Access is limited to after-school hours. Because selection is done centrally at BNLS headquarters, understanding of teacher and pupil needs is not built into the process and there is a resulting lack of knowledge as to what constitutes an effective stock. The use of local, unqualified staff keeps costs down. But if adequate support is to be given to teachers, pupils and adult users, then more qualified staff would be required – the same sort of staff that are required in the 'traditional' school library. The cost-sharing that exists at present demands that good relations continue between the different government ministries concerned. The number of Village Reading Rooms is only 64, with three scheduled to be added each year. The number of primary schools in Botswana is 759. So it will be a long time before all are served in this way.

The protagonists of joint school/community libraries see them as a way to overcome the slow development of school libraries and to reduce the fierce competition for library funding. They are also seen as a way to integrate the concept of education into the development of the whole community. Education will no longer be limited in time (school-age) and confined in space (school building) (Knuth, 1994; Tawete, 1995).

But the relevant research literature is unanimous that no real savings are realized by combining facilities (Le Roux, 1996). It is not an inexpensive solution if both school and community needs are to be met. Teachers still need to be trained in the application of information skills across the curriculum. Books have to be accessible to pupils throughout the school day. At the same time the service needs to be firmly rooted in social needs and the cultural patterns of specific communities. This calls for highly trained and specialist staff and a book stock which meets two totally different needs. The ten joint school/public libraries that were set up in Tanzania in the 1970s have not survived.

Other models

It has not been possible in this study to examine examples of all models. Learning centres are not included, although they are likely to combine the features of community resource centres and teachers resource centres. Virtual libraries and networked resources are very new to Africa at the school level and their effectiveness has not yet been evaluated.

Co-operation with other libraries was suggested in Tanzania as a way to improve school level provision. No one method of information supply should try and be self-sufficient, but rather the total resources of a country should be made available to everyone according to need.

Public libraries often see themselves as also having an educational role and try to meet needs of schools in the library's service area. An example comes from South Africa (Botham, 1996) where a public library has established a separate curriculum-related collection for school learners and encourages class visits. Book boxes are issued to schools. The READ programme also encourages teachers to introduce their pupils to the collections of bigger public libraries in nearby towns.

In Zimbabwe, the Bulawayo Public Library (Doust, 1998) offers a mobile service to primary schools in the surrounding urban area. The vehicle calls at each school on a weekly basis. It is estimated that the service costs about a quarter of what it would cost to establish and maintain a library at each school. The book stock is intensively used. The downside is that books are only available for one hour each week, so access is severely limited.

Strategies

The evidence provided by the case studies suggests that the most effective and the most cost-effective way of providing supplementary reading materials is through models which are school-based and, at least at the primary level, classroom-based. However this is not to conclude that every country in Africa should move towards providing classroom libraries in their schools. Any decision concerning school level library provision must also recognize that each model has its merits and these can be strengthened (or weakened) depending, amongst other things, on:

- the vigour of implementation;
- quality and quantity of resource material supplied;
- relevant training of teachers;
- the political and community will to fund and maintain.

Not all classroom libraries will have the success of those organized by READ, unless a similar implementing body, combining supply of materials with teacher training, community motivation, fundraising and ongoing support, is also actively engaged in promoting the programme.

- Choice of model must ultimately depend on the financial, human and material resources available in-country. It is necessary to build upon the strengths of the library services that already exist in a country and will continue to exist in the future. Gauging the available financial resources is particularly important. It is only if annual maintenance costs are within the finances of either government or the community or a combination of the two, that a model can be deemed affordable. It is pointless aiming for a one library, one school model, unless there is the finance to train and subsequently to pay for a librarian in each school. Where finance is strictly limited, then a book box model is probably the answer.

- It is not necessary to restrict choice to just one model. A combination of different models may bring about the end result of school-based resources. School libraries, classroom libraries and book box libraries all provide school-based resources. A SLS can strengthen school-based provision; so can a TRC. A public library can provide book boxes or run mobile libraries to schools.

- Within one country, it is also possible to have a multiplicity of solutions or to move from one model to another, as more finances become available. Botswana, for example, has provided schools at the senior and junior secondary level with centralized school libraries. At the primary level, needs are met by Village Reading Rooms, in community-based facilities, or by a book box service. Brazil (Andrade Antunes, 1996) has made use of reading rooms, reading corners in classrooms, circulating rack boxes (book boxes) and mobile libraries, in an attempt to equip all schools with library facilities. The present view in South Africa is that it is preferable to start with book boxes in every school and move towards the more expensive option of centralized school libraries as an ultimate goal, rather than establish a few school libraries and leave the remainder of schools with no facilities at all. The provision of modular book units in Namibian schools is also seen as a stepping stone to larger library collections (Tötemeyer, 1996).

In this research, it has proved difficult to compare the effectiveness of different models. Performance and cost data were difficult to find. Also lacking was any accepted measure of what constitutes effective provision. Unless some agreement is reached, it will always be difficult to monitor and evaluate library provision at the school level.

Possible indicators of performance are:
• number of books per pupil;
• quality of books (relevance, currency);
• use (by teachers and pupils);
• impact on student achievement.

To these must be added affordability:
• set-up costs per pupil (purchase of books, management, facility provision);
• annual maintenance costs per pupil (replacement of books, management, facility upkeep);
• costs per book per year.

If this sort of data was collected and made available, then it would be more possible for Ministries of Education or schools in Africa to make informed choices between the various models of providing access to supplementary reading materials that exist.

APPENDIX
DATA COLLECTION INSTRUMENTS

Chapter Three: School Library Services, Ghana and Tanzania

Data was collected in late 1997 by Professor A. A. Alemna, Department of Library and Archival Studies, University of Ghana and Alli Mcharazo, Tanzania Library Services, through questionnaire and interviews. This Appendix gives the data collection instrument used.

INTERVIEW FRAMEWORK

The aim is to collect data concerning the development and current and future activities of the Schools and Colleges Department (SCD) of Ghana Library Board (GLB) / School Library Service (SLS) of Tanzania Library Services (TLS).

Section A and B may be answered through consultation of annual reports and other records.

Section C will require interviews with officers of the GLB / TLS and teachers in schools/lecturers in education/ministry officials.

A DEVELOPMENT

1 Staffing
   Give the numbers of professional, para-professional and non-professional staff working in SCD / SLS for the following three years:
   1975 _____
   1985 _____
   1995 _____

2 Expenditure
   (a) Give the actual expenditure of SCD / SLS in cedis / shillings and equivalent US$ (at the rate of exchange for the year in question) for the following three years:
   1975 _____
   1985 _____
   1995 _____

(b) Give the % of total GLB / TLS recurrent expenditure that was spent on SCD / SLS for the following three years:

1975 _____

1985 _____

1995 _____

B   RECENT ACTIVITIES

3   Give the number of the following that have been undertaken or produced by SCD / SLS since 1990:

(a) advisory visits to schools _____

(b) visits by school mobile library _____

(c) lists of recommended books _____

(d) training courses for school librarians _____

(e) books/journals purchased and distributed to schools _____

(f) donated books/journals distributed to schools _____

(g) manuals on library procedures compiled _____

(h) standards _____

(i) other _____

C   PERFORMANCE

4   School Library Service

(a) In your opinion, have the activities of SCD / SLS assisted in the development of school libraries in Ghana / Tanzania? Give reasons and examples.

(b) In what ways could the performance of SCD / SLS be improved? Give examples.

(c) Are there any plans to alter the role and/or activities of SCD / SLS or to replace it with something else in the near future? How?

5   School libraries

(a) What is your opinion of the current state of school libraries in Ghana / Tanzania? Give reasons and examples.

(b) Do you consider that a school library is essential to the education process? Give reasons.

(c) How can the availability of reading materials in schools best be improved? What should be given priority at the moment?

INTERVIEW SCHEDULE

SECTION 1 — PROVISION / AVAILABILITY

SUFFICIENCY OF THE COLLECTION

1 Is the size of the classroom library (the number of items) sufficient, bearing in mind the number of pupils in your class?
2 Is there a mechanism for replenishing your library to address the pupil/book ratio if necessary? If 'yes' what is the procedure for replenishing your collection?

ACCESSIBILITY

3 How many times can a pupil access your library in one day or during a lesson? Are learners satisfied with the number of times?
4 How many items are issued out per learner and for how long can they be kept? Are learners satisfied with the length of time?

SECTION 2 — RELEVANCE

5 Are teachers involved in materials selection for their classroom libraries? If not, who is involved?
6 Does the material in your library support the curriculum? If yes, how, and if not, where are shortfalls/weaknesses in the library collection?
7 From your observation, are learners satisfied with the type of materials included in the library? If not, where are the shortfalls and which materials are not popular?
8 Do you sometimes feel the need to access other types of libraries and if so, do you access them and for what?
9 If yes to 8 above, which libraries do you access?

Any suggestions?

SECTION 3 — STAFF TRAINING

10 Who offers original training for teachers and are there any problems related to training?
11 Are there any in-service training or follow-up workshops for sustainability? If so, how often are these sessions?
12 During training are you made fully aware of the objectives of classroom libraries, and are you able to relate those objectives to those of education generally?

Any suggestions?

SECTION 4 — IMPACT

13 How long does it take learners after initiation to the library, to *access* it independently?

14 How long does it take learners to *select reference materials* and *materials for projects* independently?

15 How long do learners take to select *fiction* independently?

16 How long does it take learners to display *preferences* in relation to fiction genre, context and content?

17 How long does it take learners to start displaying a reading habit by engaging themselves with reading when not formally occupied, without the teacher's instruction?

18 How long does it take, after the initial introduction to the library, for learners to:
   - display logical and critical thinking skills?
   - to decipher differing viewpoints on a topic?
   - to criticize or challenge other viewpoints after first initiation to the library?
   - to formulate their own arguments and viewpoints and to draw their own conclusions?

19 Do you sometimes need assistance and support from READ in using your library? If yes, is that assistance easily available?

20 Do you get support from the education department for your involvement with READ, specifically the running of classroom libraries?

21 Do parents become involved in their children's reading and, if so, how? If not, where is the problem?

A TEACHER INTERVIEW

BACKGROUND INFORMATION

1 Name and address of school.
2 Name of interviewee.
3 Academic and professional qualifications.
4 How long have you taught in your present school?
5 What subjects do you teach?

USER SATISFACTION QUESTIONS

1 Do you ever use a Teachers Advisory Centre (TAC)?
2 If so, how often do you use the TAC and why?
3 If you do not use a TAC or have ceased to use it, why?
4 Do you arrange for your pupils to visit and use a TAC?
5 If so, how often do your pupils visit and use a TAC and why?
6 Does your school management, for example, the headmaster encourage and support the use of your nearest TAC by teachers and pupils?
7 Are the numbers of information materials available in the TAC that you use sufficient? Would you prefer more?
8 What type of materials do you prefer in terms of subject coverage?
9 Is the level of information materials available in accordance with your needs?
10 Are you involved in the selection of materials stocked in the TAC? If not, would you like to see any changes made?
11 Are you able to use the information materials in the TAC whenever you require to do so? If not, what changes would you like?
12 Are you provided with all the information services that you need (e.g. reference, loan, study space, enquiries, advice)? If not, what other services do you require?
13 Have you received any training in the use of materials available in the TAC in teaching?
14 Do you also use another type of library? If so, what is lacking in your TAC that makes you go searching for an alternative source(s)?
15 If you had the choice, what type of service would you prefer for obtaining the books you need to support your teaching?

1   How do you rate your pupils' performance in the Kenya Certificate of Primary Education Examinations?
2   How was the pupils' performance in the KCPE before the TAC was introduced in this zone?
3   Do you think that the TAC has resulted in or contributed to improvement of the examination pass rate in this school? Why?
4   Do you think that the abilities of pupils have changed with the introduction and use of the TAC? In what way?
5   Do you think that there has been any reduction in school drop out rate or class repetitions since the introduction and use of the TAC by teachers and pupils?
6   Do you feel that the benefits to your pupils exceed the cost of providing materials and services in the Teachers Advisory Centre?

B   ZONAL TAC TUTOR INTERVIEW

1   Name of Zone.
2   Name of interviewee.
3   Qualifications and designation.
4   Period of service with the TAC.
5   Date the TAC was established.
6   Opening hours of the TAC.
7   What is the number of persons who use the TAC in a year?
8   What types of materials are available in the TAC?
9   How many books and other information items are available in the TAC?
10 What is the range of subjects covered? How many books in Science, English, other subjects?
11 How current are the books and other materials available in the TAC?
12 How many books or other educational materials are loaned to pupils and teachers in a month? In a year?
13 What types of services are provided to pupils and teachers?
14 What is the source of funding of the TAC?
15 What problems are encountered in the running and operation of the TAC?

Chapter Eight: Village Reading Rooms, Botswana

A STAFF INTERVIEW

Location:

ABOUT YOU:

How long have you worked here?

What qualifications did you need to get your job?

What training have you had for this job?

Has your training given you enough information to help users?

What are your main duties?

ABOUT YOUR VRR:

What is the purpose of the reading room?

Does it fulfill its purpose?

Why?/How do you know this?

How long has the VRR been open?

What are the opening hours?

How many seats does it have?

Are these enough for the users?

Who uses the VRR?

ABOUT YOUR USERS:

Of the school children/students, what percentage are using the room for:
a) homework
b) other reading activities?

Apart from using the Reading Room for reading what other activities also take place here?

ABOUT YOUR STOCK:

What kinds of materials do you stock?

Who chooses the materials?

Are they the kinds of materials you need for your users?

Why?

What other kinds of materials would you like to have in the VRR?

Any other comments:

B USER INTERVIEW

Location:

ABOUT YOU:

How old are you?

Where do you go to school/study?

What standard/form are you in?

Do you have a library at school?

When do you use it?

What do you do there?

What kind of materials does it have?

Do you use any other libraries? (give details)

ABOUT THIS VRR:

How often do you come to the VRR?

Is it open when you want to use it?

Why do you come to the VRR?

What do you do in the VRR?
a) study
b) read magazines/newspapers
c) find books for study
d) find books for leisure reading
e) meet other people

If there was no VRR where would you
a) study
b) find the materials you need

Do you know others who use the VRR? (details)

What do they use it for?
a) study
b) leisure
c) as a meeting place
d) other

ABOUT THE MATERIALS IN THIS VRR:

What is good about the materials here?

Do the materials here meet your needs? Why?

What is lacking in materials here?

Do you look for materials in English or Setswana?

Any other comments:

BIBLIOGRAPHY

Abbott, C. (1994) *Performance measurement in library and information services* London: Aslib.

Abbott, C. (1996) in Rosenberg, D. (ed.) *Performance indicators: a training aid for university librarians* London: International African Institute.

Abidi, S. A. H. (ed.) (1996) *School libraries in Uganda: papers and proceedings of a DSE/EASL/MOES seminar, Kampala, 1995* Bonn: DSE.

Adams, A. and Pearce, J. (1974) *Every English teacher: a guide to English teaching for the non-specialist* Oxford: OUP.

Adams, E. (ed.) (1975) *In-service education and teachers' centres* Oxford: Pergamon Press.

Adekanmbi, A. (1998) 'Developing libraries in primary schools: reflections of a practitioner' *African Journal of Library, Archives and Information Science* 8 (1): 53–57.

Adelusi, J. O. (1998) 'A survey of library resources in secondary schools in Ekiti East Local Government, Nigeria' *Focus* 29 (1): 39–45.

ADG (Association des Documentalistes du Gabon) (1993) 'Rôle des bibliothèques scolaires au Gabon' *L'Ecluse* 5 (4): 11–12.

Aide et Action (1996) *Programme Sénégal: rapport d'activité* 51–52 Dakar: Aide et Action.

Aina, S. A. (1984) 'Stimulating the non-user' in Van der Laan, J. and Winters, A. A. (eds) *The use of information in a changing world* Amsterdam: Elsevier Science Publishers: 399–407.

Alemna, A. A. (1983) 'The development of school libraries in Ghana' *International Library Review* 15: 217–223.

Alemna, A. A. (1990) 'The school library in Ghanaian education: an analysis of issues and problems' *Nigerian Library and Information Science Review* 8 (2): 1–9.

Alemna, A. A. (1993) 'Management of school libraries in Ghana: a case for new standards' *Library Management* 14 (4): 31–35.

Alemna, A. A. (1994) *Libraries and information provision in Ghana* Accra: Type Cp. Ltd.: 36–44.

Alemna, A. A. (1996) *The future of school libraries in Ghana* (Unpublished paper)

Amaral, W. do (1994) 'Sistemas e serviços de informação em Moçambique: panoram geral Maputo' (Paper, 1st anniversary of DABA – Angolan Library Association)

ANC (African National Congress) (1995) *A policy framework for education and training* Swaziland: Macmillan Boleswa.

Anderson, R. C. (1996) 'Research foundations to support wide reading' in Greaney, V. (ed.), 55–77.

Andrade Antunes, W. de (1996) 'Brazil's experiences with mobile libraries' in Karlsson, J. (ed.)

Aparicio, A. (1997) 'Libraries and the publishing sector in Angola' *African Publishing Review* 6 (2): 8–9.

Apeji, E. A. (1997) 'Developments in education, libraries and book publishing in Nigeria' *Education Libraries Journal* 40 (1): 9–15.

Ayot, H. (1983) 'Teacher Advisory Centres in Kenya' in Greenland, J. (ed.) *The in-service training of primary school teachers in English speaking Africa* London: Macmillan.

Baffour-Awuah, M. (1998) 'School libraries in Botswana: a state of the art report' *School Libraries Worldwide* 4 (2): 22–33.

Baker, P. (1994) 'Books – what books? A library in a South African school for black children' *School Librarian* 4 (4): 136, 141.

Balock, L. (1997) 'Bibliothèques et services de documentation au Cameroon: un chemin long à parcourir: deuxième partie (suite et fin)' *L'Ecluse* 9 (2): 13–14.

Baine, D. and Mwamwenda, T. (1994) 'Education in Southern Africa: current conditions and future directions' *International Review of Education* 40 (2): 113–134.

Bawa, R. (1993) 'The future of school libraries in South Africa' *Education Libraries Journal* 36 (1):7–17.

Bawa, R. (1996) 'An implementation plan for the development of school libraries in the KwaZulu–Natal region' PhD Thesis: Pietermaritzburg: University of Natal, Department of Information Studies.

Behrens, S. J. (1995) 'Lifelong learning in the new education and training system' *Mousaion* 13 (1 and 2): 250–263.

Bennett, R. (1991) 'Criteria for successful children's books in South Africa' in *Book publishing in South Africa for the 1990s: proceedings of a symposium held at the South African Library, Cape Town, 22–25 November, 1989* Cape Town: South African Library.

Berhane, G. (1996) Letter in *Link-Up* 8 (4): 4.

Berkowitz, R. E. (1994) 'From indicators of quantity to measures of effectiveness: ensuring Information Power's mission' in Kuhlthau, C. C. (ed.) *Assessment and the school library media centre* Englewood, Col.: Libraries Unlimited: 33–42.

Blacquiere, A. (1989) 'Reading for survival: text and the second language student' *South African Journal of Higher Education* 3 (1): 73–82.

BLD (1998) *Bibliothèque, Lecture, Développement, 1994–1997* Dakar: BLD.

Botham, D. (1996) 'Structured public library information services to school learners: the case of Belhar Public Library, Cape Town' in Karlsson, J. (ed.): 81–85.

Botswana Economic Snapshot: *Botswana economy facts and figures* <http://www.gov.bw/economy/index.html>

Botswana, (1991) Ministry of Finance and Development Planning *National Development Plan 7 1991/92-1996/97* (NDP7).

Botswana, (1993) National Commission on Education *Report.*

Botswana (1994) *Revised National Policy on Education* Government paper; no. 2.

Botswana, (1997) Ministry of Finance and Development Planning *National Development Plan 8 1997/98-2002/03* (NDP8).

Botswana, (1997) Ministry of Local Government and Lands *Kgatleng District Development Plan 5 1997-2003.*

Botswana National Library Service (1998) *Brochure.*

Brindley, D. (1991) 'Which books do black students want to read?' *Crux* 25 (1): 58–61.

Buchan, A. (1992) 'Book development in the Third World: the British experience' in: Altbach, P. G. (ed.) *Publishing and development in the Third World* London: Hans Zell: 349–363.

Buchan, A. (1995) 'Books and information for schools in the developing world' Paper presented at the IBD/IFLA seminar, Harrogate.

Bugembe, M. H. (1998) 'The Pan-African Children's Book Fair celebrates seven years' *Bellagio Publishing Network Newsletter* 23: 7–8.

Byaruhanga, A. (1972) 'Uganda School Libraries Association's primary school book-box scheme' *Ugandan Libraries* 1 (1): 7–9.

Callison, D. (1994) 'Expanding the evaluation role in the critical-thinking curriculum' in Kuhlthau, C. C. (ed.) *Assessment and the school library media centre* Englewood, Col.: Libraries Unlimited.

Carpenter, J. and Kemp, I. in collaboration with Mascarenhas, O. (1989) *Interim report* Tanzania Books Subsector Study (Libraries and Information Section).

Carpenter, J. et al. (1990) *The book sector in Zambian education: a study prepared for the Delegate of the Commission of the European Communities and the Government of the Republic of Zambia* (Unpublished report).

Centre for Education Policy Development (CEPD) (1994) *Summary report of the IPET task teams* Johannesburg: CEPD.

Centre for Educational Technology and Distance Education (1997) *A national policy framework for school library standards* Pretoria: Department of Education.

Chakava, H. (1998) 'Kenya: a decade of African publishing for children, 1988–1998' Paper presented at Indaba, Zimbabwe International Book Fair, Harare.

Colbert, V., Chiappe, C. and Arboleda, J. (199?) *The New School program: more and better primary education for children in rural areas in Colombia*

Committee on Teacher Education Policy (COTEP) (1995) *Norms and standards and governance structure for teacher education* Pretoria: Department of Education.

Corréa, A. (1997) 'Book hunger in schools' *Focus* 28 (2): 90–91.

Côte d'Ivoire (1997) Ministère de L'Education Nationale et de la Formation de Base 'La lecture en Côte d'Ivoire' Paper presented at a Regional Seminar on Training of Trainers, Dakar, 1997.

Culling, G. (1974) 'Introduction to teachers centres' in *Educational Development International*.

Daily News, Gaborone: Botswana Press Agency.

Dawit, M. (1998) 'A school library in Ethiopia' *Link-Up* 10 (1): 6–8.

Day, C. (1993) 'Open group discussions as a market research method' *Library Association Record* 93 (6): 389–90, 92.

'De la scolarisation des filles au Mali' (1987) *Jamana*, 13: 36–43.

de Villiers, A. P. (1997) 'Inefficiency and the demographic realities of the South African school system' *South African Journal of Education* 17 (2): 76–81.

Diakiw, J. Y. (1990) 'Children's literature and global education: understanding the developing world' *The Reading Teacher* 43 (4): 296–300.

Diallo, M. (1993) 'Réflexion sur l'école malienne' *Jamana* (Malian cultural review), 34: 10–14.

Diop, M. B. and Kabou, E. (1992) 'Vie de L'ASBAD: enquête nationale sur les bibliothèques scolaires' *L'Ecluse* 7 (2): 11–13.

Doll, C. A. (1997) 'Quality and elementary school library media collections' *School Library Media Quarterly* 25 (2): 95–101.

Doust, R. W. (1998) 'Provision of school library services by means of mobile libraries – the Zimbabwe experience' Paper presented to 64th IFLA General Conference, Amsterdam, 16–21 August.

Education Foundation (1997) *EduSource Data News* 17 August: 3.

Elley, W. B. (1996) 'Using book floods to raise literacy levels in developing countries' in Greaney, V. (ed.), 148–162.

Faye, D. (1998) 'Books and children: the 1998 Indaba at the Zimbabwe International Book Fair' *Bellagio Publishing Network Newsletter* 23: 5–6.

Feather, J. and Sturges, P. (1996) (eds) *International encyclopedia of information and library science* London: Routledge.

Ferguson, M. J. (1929) *Memorandum: libraries in the Union of South Africa, Rhodesia and Kenya Colony* New York: Carnegie Corporation of New York.

Field, W. (1999) 'In the city of flowers' *Library Association Record* 101 (4): 230–231.

Ford, G. (1988) 'Approaches to performance measurement: some observations on principles and practice' *British Journal of Academic Librarianship* 3 (1): 74–87.

Francis, M. (1989) 'In my opinion...: central or classroom collections?' *School Librarian* 37 (1): 13.

Fremy, D. and M. (1993) *QUID 1994*. Paris: Editions Robert Laffont: 1076–1077.

Frost, E. (1972) 'School library service in Tanzania' *East African Library Association Bulletin* 13: 113–117.

Fuller, B. (1986) 'Raising school quality in developing countries: what investment boosts learning' *Discussion Paper No. 1* Washington: World Bank.

Gazza, S. (1997) *Les habitudes de lecture en Afrique sub-Saharienne et les apprentissages traditionnels: bibliographie analytique* London: ADEA.

Gibbs, S. E. (1985) 'The library as an attitude of mind: the role of the library in the primary school' *School Librarian* 33 (4): 309–315.

Greaney, V. (ed.) (1996) *Promoting reading in developing countries* Newark, Del.: International Reading Association.

Hanna, G. R. (1965) *Books, young people and reading guidance* New York: Harper and Row.

Higgs, P. (1994) 'Education or socialisation: a dilemma for philosophy of education' *Acta Academica* 26 (1): 88–103.

Higgs, P. (1997) 'A re-vision of philosophy of education in South African education' *South African Journal of Education* 17 (3): 100–107.

Hockey, S. W. (1960) *Development of library services in East Africa: a report submitted to the governments of East Africa* (Unpublished report).

Hugo, C. (1996) 'Classroom libraries' in Karlsson, J. (ed.): 87–90.

Hugo, C. D. (1998) 'Strategies to promote children's books and reading development: sharing the READ experience' Paper presented at Indaba, Zimbabwe International Book Fair, Harare.

Hurst, L. (1993) 'The responses of children to the elements of humour and justice in stories: a cross-cultural perspective' MEd Thesis: Pietermaritzburg: University of Natal, Department of Education.

Hutcheson, A. M. (1998) 'South Africa' in *Africa South of the Sahara, 27th edition* London: Europa Publications Limited.

Hüttemann, L. and Ng'ang'a, S. K. (eds) (1990) *Co-ordination of information systems and services in Kenya* Bonn: DSE.

Ikiara, G. K. (1988) 'The economy' in *Kenya: an official handbook* Nairobi: Ministry of Information and Broadcasting: 59–87.

Ilomo, C. S. (1985) 'Towards more effective school library programmes in Tanzania' *Occasional Papers*, No. 23 Dar es Salaam: Tanzania Library Services.

Institut Pédagogique National (1979) *Deuxième Séminaire sur l'Education: documents préparatoires* Bamako: IPN.

International Consultative Forum on Education for All (1998) 'Wasted opportunities: when schools fail: repetition and drop-out in primary schools' *Education for All: status and trends* Paris: UNESCO.

Isaacman, J. (1996) *Understanding the National Qualifications Framework: a guide to life-long learning* Johannesburg: Heinemann.

Johnson, I. M. (1995) 'International issues in school librarianship: the IFLA Pre-Session Seminar, 1993' *Information Development* 11 (1): 50–55.

Jorosi, B. N. (1997) 'Community school libraries in Botswana: impressions of the contemporary scene' *Education Libraries Journal* 40 (3): 23–28.

Kahn, H. (1991) *Teachers' resource centres* London: Commonwealth Secretariat.

Kalusopa, T and Chifwepa, V. (1997) 'Secondary school libraries in Zambia: dream or reality?' A case study of the Copperbelt Province, Lusaka.

Kamfer, L. (1989) 'Focus groups in organizational research' *Journal of Industrial Psychology* 15 (1): 7–12.

Kaniki, A. M. (1997) 'Continuing education and training programmes for library and information personnel in South Africa's educational institutions' *Education for Information* 15 (1): 1–15.

Karlsson, J. (ed.) (1996) *School learners and libraries* Dalbridge, S. A.: Education Policy Unit, University of Natal.

Karlsson, J., Nassimbeni, M. and Karelse, C-M. (1996) 'Identifying the inherited problems in the provision of resources for school learners' in Karlsson, J. (ed.).

Kaungamno, E. E. (1974) 'School libraries as a basic tool for teaching' *Tanzania Education Journal* 3: 38–40. Paper delivered to International Association of School Librarianship Conference, Nairobi, 1973.

Kaungamno, E. E. (1981) 'Tanzania' in Jackson, M. M. *Contemporary developments in librarianship: an international handbook* London: Library Association: 108–109.

Kaungamno, E. E. and Ilomo, C. S. (1979) *Books build nations, Vol. 1: Library services in West and East Africa* London: Transafrica; Dar es Salaam: Tanzania Library Services: 39.

Kaungamno, E. E. and Ilomo, C. S. (1979) *Books build nations, Vol. 2: Library services in Tanzania* London: Transafrica; Dar es Salaam: Tanzania Library Services: 194–197.

Keita, M. K. (1989) *Les structures en matière d'information du Ministère des Sports, des Arts et de la Culture et leurs perspectives* Bamako.

Kenya Library Association (1986) *School libraries in Kenya: policy guidelines.*

Kenya (1995) *Statistical abstract* Ministry of Planning and National Development, Central Bureau of Statistics: Nairobi.

Kenya (1994) *Demographic and health survey* Ministry of Home Affairs and National Heritage, National Council for Population and Development: Nairobi.

Kinnell, M. (ed.) (1992) *Learning resources in schools: Library Association Guidelines for School Libraries* London: LA Publishing.

Kinyanjui, P. and Gakuru, O. N. (1988) 'Education and manpower development' in *Kenya: an official handbook* Nairobi: Ministry of Information and Broadcasting: 135–153.

Klynsmith, J. T. O. (1993) 'School library services in Namibia' in *Co-ordination of Information Systems and Services in Namibia: papers of the seminar held in Windhoek, 1993* Bonn: DSE: 172–182.

Knuth, R. (1994) 'Libraries, literacy and development: combined libraries as an option for developing countries: a brief communication' *International Information and Library Review* 26: 77–89.

Konaté Sié (1994) 'Dénonce l'absence de volonté politique en Afrique' *L'Ecluse* 6(3): 9–10.

Kotei, S. I. A. and Milazi, D. B. T. (1984) *National Book Policy for Botswana: investigation of reading habits and book needs among literates and semi-literates* Gaborone: University of Botswana.

Kraft, R. J. (1998) *Rural educational reform in the Nueva Escuela Unitaria of Guatemala* Washington: AED, USAID.

Kramiller, G. and Fairhurst, G. (1999) *The effectiveness of teacher resource centre strategy* (Education Research; Serial no. 34) London: DFID.

Krige, D. et al. (1995) 'Mapping education' *Indicator South Africa* 12 (2): 76–80.

Kruger, J. A. (1981) 'School Library Service [Republic of South Africa]' in Jackson, M. M. *Contemporary developments in librarianship: an international handbook* London: Library Association: 96–103.

Kuhlthau, C.C. (1993) 'Implementing a process approach to information skills: a study identifying indicators of success in library media programmes' *School Library Media Quarterly* 22 (1): 11–18.

Kutoane, K. I. and Kruger, R. A. 'The need for a culture-based curriculum design for black schools' *Educamus* 36 (10): 8–12.

Le Roux, N. and Schollar, E. (1996) *A survey report on the reading and writing skills of pupils participating in READ programmes* Braamfontein: READ.

Le Roux, S. (1996) 'The school/community library concept' in Karlsson, J. (ed.).

Leeb, W. (1990) 'They have a dream' *NU Focus* 1 (2): 30.

Mali (1993) Direction Nationale de la Statistique et de l'Informatique *Quelques Statistiques du Mali* Bamako: DNSI.

Mali (1995) Direction Nationale de la Statistique et de l'Informatique *Annuaire Statistique du Mali* 1995 Bamako: DNSI.

Mali (1996) Direction Nationale de la Statistique et de l'Informatique *Flash Statistique* Bamako: DNSI.

Mali (1996) Ministère de l'Education de Base *Guide des Nouvelles Pistes* Bamako, AMAP.

Markless, S. (1986) 'Towards an information skills network' *School Librarian* 34 (1): 21–25.

Martins, Z., Zacarias, F. and Matavele, J. (1993) *Avaliação intermédia do projecto 'Criação de um ambiente de leitura em Cabo Delgado'* Maputo, Moçambique: Instituto Nacional de Desenvolvimento da Educação.

Masagara, E. M. (1983) 'The role of Teachers Advisory Centres in the education of teachers in Kenya: a case study of Nandi District' PGDE Thesis, Nairobi: Kenyatta University.

Masiga, E. S. (1989) 'The need for a school library policy in Kenya, its relevance, obstacles and suggested solutions' Paper presented to the Kenya Library Association Annual Seminar, 21 to 24 February.

Maximiano, E. (1996) *Síntese das visitas às províncias* Maputo: Ministério da Educação, Centro de Documentação.

McEwan, P. J. (1995) *Primary school reform for rural development: an evaluation of Colombian New Schools.*

McGregor, C., Mortimer, K. and Lister, T. (1990) *Study on book provision in Kenyan education* London: Latimer Lion.

Mchombu, K. J. and Muttanyatta, J. N. S. (1987) *The Village Reading Room Pilot Project: an evaluation* Gaborone: Botswana National Library Service.

Minzi, L. D. T. (1999) Personal communication with the author.

Mndambi, M. S. G. (1998) 'The Children's Book Project' *African Publishing Review* 7 (2): 16.

Moshi, E. (1998) 'Books and children in Tanzania' Paper presented at Indaba, Zimbabwe International Book Fair, Harare.

Mozambique (1997) *Moçambique.em números 1996: Mozambique in figures 1996* Maputo: Instituto Nacional de Estatística.

Mozambique (1994) *Indicadores educacionais e efectivos escolares: ensino primário, 1983–1992* Maputo: Ministério da Educação.

Mozambique (1994) *Indicadores educacionais e efectivos escolares: ensino primário, 1993–1994, ension secundário geral, 1983–1994* Maputo: Ministério da Educação.

Mozambique (1996) *Política para a constituição, apetrechamento e melhoramento das bibliotecas escolares* Maputo: Ministério da Educação.

Mulaha, A. K. (1983) 'The evolvement of school libraries in Kenya' *International Library Review* 15: 207–215.

Mulaha, A. K. (1986) 'School librarianship in Kenya' Paper presented to the Kenya Library Association Annual Seminar, 12 to 14 February.

Munoko, F. K. (1996) 'Teachers' Resource Centres: their role in Kenyan secondary schools: a case study of Bukembe Teachers' Resource Centre, Bungoma District' MPhil thesis, Moi University: Kenya.

Musisi, J. S. (1993) 'School libraries in Kenya' in Anwar, M. A. *et al* (eds) *Library and information services in developing countries: a festschrift for Anis Khurshid* Lahore: Library & Information Management Academy: 150–161.

Mutanyatta, J. N. S. and Mchombu, K. J. (1995) *The Village Reading Room services in Botswana: final report of an evaluative study* Gaborone: Botswana National Library Service.

Nardi, M. (1998) 'Au Bénin: une biblio-pirogue sur le lac Nokou au Bénin' *Takam Tikou* 7: 9–10.

Nawatsi, W. W. (1997) *Personal memorandum* 5 October.

Ndiaye, E. (1996) 'Les bibliothèques à double circuit au Sénégal' *Notre Librarie* Juin: 106–109.

NEPI (National Education Policy Investigation) (1992) *Library and information services: report of the NEPI Library and Information Services Research Group* Cape Town: OUP/NECC.

Niconte, M. B. (1994) *Visita de trabalho às províncias de Nampula e Cabo Delgado: relatório final* Maputo: Ministério da Educação, Centro de Documentação.

Nkomo, M. (ed.) (1990) *Pedagogy of domination: toward a democratic education in South Africa* Trenton, NJ: Africa World Press, Inc.

Norton, D.E. (1991) *Through the eyes of the child: an introduction to children's literature, 3rd edition* New York: Macmillan.

Nwoye, S. C. (1981) 'Nigeria' in Jackson, M. M. *International handbook of contemporary developments in librarianship, Part 1: Africa* Westport, Conn.: Greenwood Press: 51–69.

Oberg, D. and Easton, E. (1995) 'Focus group interviews: a tool for program evaluation in school library education' *Education for Information* 13: 117–129.

Ocholla, D. N. (1992) 'Essentials for school library development: some worthwhile considerations for an African nation' *New Library World* 93 (1103): 9–15.

Oddoye, D. E. M. (1969) 'The role of the school library in education' *Ghana Library Journal* 3 (2): 6–10.

Odede, E. A. (1982) 'The role of Teachers Advisory Centres in the qualitative improvement of teacher education in Kenya' PGDE Thesis, Nairobi: Kenyatta University.

Odhiambo, B. D. (1995) *Teachers Advisory Centres: a brief* Nairobi: Inspectorate Section, Ministry of Education.

Odini, C. (1993) 'An overview of information systems in Kenya' *Library Review* 42 (5): 44–49.

Ofori, A. G. T. (1981) 'Ghana' in Jackson, M. M. *Contemporary developments in librarianship: an international handbook* London: Library Association: 5–7.

Ogomo, C. B. (1988) 'Teachers Advisory Centres: their role and management' Paper presented at the Training of Trainers Seminar held at Machakos from 24–28 October, 1988.

Ojiambo, J. B. (1988) 'School library services in sub-Saharan Africa' *International Library Review* 3 (3):143–155.

Olden, A. (1995) *Libraries in Africa: pioneers, policies, problems* Lanham, Md. and London: Scarecrow Press.

Oliveira, J. (1996) 'Textbooks in developing countries' in Greaney, V. (ed.), 78–90.

Orr, R. H. (1993) 'Measuring the goodness of library services: a general framework for considering quantitative measures' *Journal of Documentation* 29: 315–332.

Osei-Bonsu, M. (1990) 'Secondary school libraries in Ghana: an evaluative study' *International Review of Children's Literature and Libraries* 5 (2): 87–105.

Politique nationale des bibliothèques scolaires au Sénégal (1994) *L'Ecluse* 6 (4):12–13.

Primary Extension Reading Project: pilot project (1998) *Project manual* Buea: Teachers Resource Centre.

Promoção de um ambiente de leitura em Cabo Delgado: relatório final (1995) Maputo: Instituto Nacional de Desenvolvimento da Educação.

Psacharopoulos, G., Rojas, C. and Velez, E. (1989) *Achievement evaluation of Colombia's Escuela Nueva: is multigrade the answer?*

Radebe, T. (1994) 'Training school librarians in South Africa: a personal view' *Innovation* 9: 43–47.

Radebe, T. (1995) 'An investigation of the reading interests of Zulu speaking standard two children in the Department of Education and Training in the Pietermaritzburg 1 Circuit' MIS Thesis, Pietermaritzburg: University of Natal, Department of Information Studies.

Radebe, T. (1996a) 'Context and culture as a factor in black children's responses to books' in Machet, M., Olën, S. and van der Walt, T. (eds) *Other worlds other lives: children's literature experiences: proceedings of the International Conference on Children's Literature* 4–6 April 1995. Vol. 1: 184–202.

Radebe, T. (1996b) 'The school library movement in South Africa: recent policies and developments' in Abidi, S.A.H. (ed.).

Radebe, T. (1997) 'Experiences of teacher-librarians in the workplace after completion of the school librarianship programme' *South African Journal of Library and Information Science* 65 (4): 218.

Ray, S. (1994) 'Towards the ideal: library skills and the school library' *School Librarian* 42 (1): 8–9.

READ Educational Trust (1991, 1992, 1993, 1994, 1995, 1996, 1997) *Annual Report* Braamfontein: READ.

Read, A. (1992) 'International experiences in Third World publishing development with particular reference to World Bank interventions' in Altbach, P. G. (ed.) *Publishing and development in the Third World* London: Hans Zell: 307–324.

Relatório da componente de formação pedagógica, do projecto 'Melhoria do ensino da leitura', Cabo Delgado e Niassa, referente ao perfodo Nov. 1995 /Mar. 1997 (1997) Maputo.

Robinson, H. M. and Weintraub, S. (1973) 'Research related to children's interests and to developmental values of reading' *Library Trends* 22 (2): 81–108.

Rodríguez-Trujillo, N. (1996) 'Promoting independent reading: Venezuelan and Colombian experience' in Greaney, V. (ed.), 109–129.

Rosenberg, D. (ed.) (1998) *Getting books to school pupils in Africa: case studies* (Education Research; Serial no. 26) London: DFID.

SABAP (South African Book Aid Project) (1998) *Evaluation report: phase one* Eastern Cape Province. (Unpublished report).

Sall, A. B. (1986) 'Quelques réflexions sur le système éducatif malien' *Jamana* 10: 24–28.

Salzard, S. and Cosson, A. (1996) 'Ecole 2000: un reseau de bibliothèques scolaires en Côte d'Ivoire' *Notre Librarie* June: 104–105.

Samuelson, J. (1997) 'South Africa Book Aid Project' *Focus* 28 (2): 92–95.

Schonell, F. J. (1961) *The psychology and teaching of reading* Edinburgh: Oliver and Boyd.

School Library Services 'LEAs lose control' *Library Association Record* (1998) 100 (11): 566.

SchoolNet SA (1998) *Annual report* <http://www.school.za>

Searle, B. (1985) *General operational review of textbooks* Washington; World Bank, Education and Training Department.

SIAPAC-Africa (1992) *An evaluation of the book box service* (Prepared for Botswana National Library Service).

Sidiropoulus, E. (1997) *South African survey, 1996/1997* Johannesburg: South African Institute of Race Relations.

Sikhosana, M. (1993) in Pela, M. 'Focus on culture' *Sowetan* 29 December 1993.

Sistema Nacional de Educação: linhas gerais; lei. (1985) Maputo: Ministério da Educação.

Smith, K. (1978) 'Books and development in Africa – access and role' *Library Trends* 26 (4):469–487.

Smith, K. P. (1993) 'The multicultural ethic and connections to literature for children and young adults' *Library Trends* 41 (3): 340–353.

Songa, P. W. (1996) 'Current trends in school library development in Uganda' in Abidi, S. A. H. (ed.).

South Africa, Central Statistical Service (CSS) (1997) *Census 1996: prelimi-nary estimates of the size of the population of South Africa* Pretoria: Central Statistics Service.

South Africa (1995) *White paper on education and training* Pretoria: Department of Education.

South Africa (1997a) *Curriculum 2005: lifelong learning for the 21st Century* Pretoria: Department of Education.

South Africa (1997b) *A national policy framework for school library stan-dards: a discussion document* Pretoria: Department of Education.

Soy Zonal Teachers Advisory Centre (1992) *Annual report* Nairobi: Inspectorate Section, Ministry of Education.

Sri Lanka, Department of Primary Education (1996) *Books in schools: a project to develop English education in primary classes in Sri Lanka* Colombo: National Institute of Education.

Stadler, C. (1992) 'Rural school-library provision: gross inequalities' *Matlhasedi* 11 (2): 44–46.

Stilwell, C. (1995) 'An analysis of staff perceptions of the structure of the provincial library services and their affiliated public libraries in the light of socio-political circumstances, 1990–April 1994' PhD Thesis, Pietermaritzburg: University of Natal, Information Studies Department.

Sturges, P. and Neill, R. (1998) *The quiet struggle: information and libraries for the people of Africa, second edition* London, Washington: Mansell.

Tameem, J. A. (1992) 'A model for evaluating user satisfaction with govern-ment libraries in Saudi Arabia' *New Library World* 93 (1103): 16–22.

Tastad, S. A. and Collins, N. D. (1997) 'Teaching the information skills process and the writing process: bridging the gap' *School Library Media Quarterly* 25(3): 167–169.

Tawete, F. (1991) 'The plight of school libraries in Africa' *Information Trends* 4 (3): 123–138.

Tawete, F. (1995) 'Joint school/public libraries: a catalyst for school library development in Africa' *African Journal of Library, Archives and Information Science* 5 (1): 31–38.

Taylor, M. (1975) 'My experience with Tanzania Library Services' *Someni* 4 (1): 20–30.

Taylor, N. (1993) *Future directions for faculties of education in South Africa* Pretoria: University of South Africa.

'Teachers Resource Centre: an evaluation report from the survey of Uasin Gishu secondary schools' Report presented to Moi University Faculty of Information Sciences as part of the BSc in Information Sciences, 1992 (Unpublished paper).

The World Book, vol. 13 (1994) Chicago: World Book Inc.

Tötemeyer, A-J. (1984) 'The racial element in Afrikaans children's and youth literature' PhD Thesis, Stellenbosch: Stellenbosch University, Library Science Department.

Tötemeyer, A-J. (1993) 'Findings and recommendations of research reports on school, public, government, parastatal, private and training institution libraries and information services in Namibia' in *Co-ordination of infor-mation systems and services in Namibia* Bonn: DSE.

Tötemeyer, A-J. (1996) 'School library development policy in Namibia' in Abidi, S. A. H. (ed.) 21–34.

Toure, S. W. (1996) 'La dynamique de la lecture au Mali' *Jamana* 1: 15–19.

Traore, Mamadou (ed.) (1996) *Atlas du Mali* Paris: Les Editions J. A.

Tucker, N. (1981) *The child and the book: a psychological and literary explo-ration* Cambridge: Cambridge University Press.

Turbo Zone Teachers Advisory Centre (1993) *Annual report* Nairobi: Inspectorate Section, Ministry of Education.

UNESCO *Statistical yearbook* <http://www.unescostat.unesco.org>

UNESCO/IFLA (1998) *School library manifesto* <http://www.unesco.org> Also reprinted in *IFLA Journal* 25 (2), 1999: 116–117.

Van House, N. A. and Childers, T. A. (1993) *The public library effectiveness study: the complete report* Chicago: American Library Association.

Walker, C. M. (1993) 'From Carnegie to NEPI: ideals and realities' *Mousaion* 11 (2): 58–83.

Widdows, R., Hensler, T. A. and Wyncott, M H. (1991) 'The focus group interview: a method for assessing users' evaluation of library service' *College and Research Libraries* 52: 352–359.

Willemse, J. (1989) 'Library effectiveness: the need for measurement' *South African Journal of Library and Information Science* 57 (3): 261–266.

Wininga, F. (1999) Private communication with author.

Williams, E. (1998) *Investigating bilingual literacy: evidence from Malawi and Zambia* (Education Research Serial no. 24) London: DFID.

World Bank (1988) *Education in Sub-Saharan Africa: policies for adjustment, revitalization and expansion* Washington: World Bank.

World Bank (1990) 'Implementing education policies in Kenya' *African Technical Series Report* no. 85 Washington: World Bank.

Wyley, C. H. (1997) 'The application of a participatory evaluation method to the public library: the case of Tholulwazi Library, Besters Camp, Inanda, Durban' MIS Thesis, Pietermaritzburg: University of Natal, Department of Information Studies.

INDEX

home book loans 76-77, 172
INSET 66, 68, 86, 119-120, 157
student book accessibility 79, 82,
102-103
Teachers Advisory Centres (Kenya)
accessibility 125-127, 131, 174
collections 124-125, 131
cost-effectiveness 128-129
educational effectiveness 129-130,
153
establishment 117, 118-120
finance 119, 127, 166
independent learning 132
loans 128
objectives 121
supplementary reading material
128
travel constraints 119
tutors 118, 125-126
teacher relationship 126, 131
training 119, 131, 152, 153, 157,
174
usage 126-128
zonal centres 119
teachers' training courses 33, 34
textbooks
provision, World Bank 27
replacement by study guides 5
as supplementary readers 5
transport, limitations 110, 119, 164,
173
twin towns/cities 45, 58

Uganda 19, 22
UNESCO 5-6, 18, 27, 31, 33-34
UNICEF 119

Village Reading Rooms (Botswana)
accommodation 144, 148
advantages 175
community involvement 138, 140-
141
cost-effectiveness 146-147
educational effectiveness 146
fiction, demand for 143-144
finance 147, 148-149, 166-167
history 137-138
location 139, 144-145
materials 139, 140, 175
in Setswana 139, 140, 143
objectives 138
primary school usage 140-141, 143
research methodology 141-142
school/community provision 139
staff 139-140, 144
virtual libraries 8, 176
Voluntary Service Overseas 117-118

World Bank 24, 27

Zambia 18, 21
Zanzibar 24
Zimbabwe 21